THIRTY FAVORITE
BIBLE STORIES
for Boys and Girls

by
John Calvin Reid

illustrated by
James E. Seward

STANDARD PUBLISHING
Cincinnati, Ohio   3373

DEDICATION

To Marty, Meara, and Jonathan
by their loving grandfather

Library of Congress Cataloging in Publication Data

Reid, John Calvin, 1901-
  Thirty favorite Bible stories for boys and girls.

  Summary: A collection of Bible stories, each
accompanied by an introduction, brief prayer, and
discussion questions.
  1. Bible stories, English. [1. Bible stories]
I. Seward, James E., ill.   II. Title.
BS551.2.R4   220.9'505   81-21514
ISBN 0-87239-498-0   AACR2

PREFACE

In retelling these stories of the Bible, my first aim has been to make them *interesting*. To capture and hold the attention of children, I have given free rein to imagination, being careful all the while to observe a reverent regard for the inspired original record.

My second aim has been to make them *practical*. This is the reason for the lead-in introduction, the brief prayer, and the questions for discussion provided with each story. It is hoped that this format will help teachers and students in the classroom, as well as parents and children in the home, to discover and apply the important spiritual and moral truths which lie, partly revealed and partly concealed, between the lines of each story.

In short, these stories are intended to *teach,* as well as to *entertain!*

J. C. R.

CONTENTS

*For this story, the author has researched
first-century Jewish customs and the histori-
cal and geographical conditions in and around
Nazareth.

INTRODUCTION

In my boyhood days,
Which long ago sped,
A Bible with pictures,
Was beside my bed.

Each night a chapter
I tried to read;
Thus in my heart
To plant a good seed.

Some pages seemed dull,
I must admit;
But others so lively,
'Twas hard to quit.

The stories I liked,
I've rewritten for you;
I hope you'll love them,
As I still do.

The Author.

Chapter One

THE FIRST RAINBOW

What is the most beautiful sight you have ever seen in the sky? A rainbow? The next time you see a bright one, try to count the colors. There should be seven: red, orange, yellow, green, blue, indigo,and purple.

Do you know what makes a rainbow? Not rain by itself, but the sun shining through the rain after the cloud has passed on. So the rainbow is usually a sign that the rain is over. But once the rainbow meant much more to people who saw it.

★ ★ ★ ★ ★ ★ ★ ★

Suppose you were an artist and had finished a beautiful picture. Then suppose something bad happened to it—suppose someone broke in and splashed paint all over it! What would you do with your ruined picture? You would probably throw it away and start over, wouldn't you? According to the Bible, there was a time when God felt very much the same way about the world He had made.

At the beginning, everything was lovely, and God was pleased. The Bible says it like this: "God looked upon everything that He had made, and, behold, it was very good."

But later, people became very wicked. Not only were they wicked in what they did and said, but even their thoughts were evil. They hated one another. God felt very sad about this and decided to send a flood to destroy the world and start over.

But there was one man who was not wicked. Noah was his name. He obeyed God's commandments, taught them to his children, and lived close to God every day.

So God said to him, "Noah, there is too much hate and violence in the world. I am going to send a flood to destroy it. But because you are a good man and have always obeyed my commandments, I am going to save you and your family. Listen as I tell you what to do."

Then God told Noah to get busy and build a ship, which in those days was called an "ark." He told him what kind of wood to use, what size to make it, and how to seal it with tar so it would float when the flood came.

So Noah and his sons began building the ark. His neighbors made fun of him and called him names as they watched him and his sons working on the ark day after day, year after year, and talking about a flood coming when there was not a cloud in the sky. But that didn't bother Noah. He knew he was doing what God had told him to do.

After a while, the ark was finished. God told Noah to get in a supply of food, and also to take into the ark animals and birds of every kind, both males and females, so these would not drown in the flood.

In all these things, Noah did exactly as God told him. Then he and his wife and his three sons and their wives went into the ark, and God shut the door.

Before long, the clouds came and the rain began to fall. In great torrents, it kept pouring down for forty days and forty nights until everywhere the land was covered. Even the mountains were under water. When at last the rain stopped and the skies cleared, there was no land to be seen anywhere. But the ark still floated safely on top of the water.

Finally, the ark landed on a mountain called Ararat. Noah waited two months to let the water drain away from the earth. Then he sent out a dove to find out if the waters had dried up. The dove flew here and there, but could find no place to land; so she returned to the ark.

Noah waited another week, then sent the dove out again. Late that evening, she came back, this time with an olive leaf in her mouth. So Noah and his family knew the waters were beginning to dry up and the land to appear. Again Noah waited a week and sent the dove out a third time. This time she did not return. The land was dry!

Then God said to Noah, "Go out now, you and your family and also all the birds and animals that have been kept alive from the flood." So Noah opened the door, and out came the animals and the birds. Then he and his family came out too.

Can you guess the first thing they did? They built an altar and prepared to pray because they were so grateful! Then, kneeling around the altar, they thanked God for His great kindness in saving them from the flood.

When they finished praying, they looked up, and what do you suppose they saw in the sky? A glorious rainbow!

And God said to Noah, "The rainbow is a sign of the promise I now make to you and your children, that never again will there be a flood that will destroy the whole earth. While the world lasts, there will be a sowing time and harvest, summer and winter, and day and night. The rainbow is my sign that I will keep my promise."

So to Noah and his family, and to all people since, the rainbow has been and still is a sign of God's promise that never again will the earth be destroyed by a flood. The next time you see a beautiful rainbow in the sky, remember what it means.

Prayer

Dear God, how many beautiful things there are in the world around us and in the sky

Noah's Family Thanks God

above us that speak to us of Your greatness, Your power, and Your love!

Help us, not only to notice these things, but to praise You for them and to be truly thankful for Your great goodness to us. In Jesus' name, amen.

★ ★ ★ ★ ★ ★ ★ ★

QUESTIONS ON CHAPTER ONE

1. How did God feel about the wickedness He saw in the world in the time of Noah?
2. How was Noah different from the other people who lived at that time?
3. Do you think those people could have done something that might have influenced God to "change His mind" and not send the flood? If so, what? (See Jonah, Chapter 3.)
4. How do you think God feels about the wickedness He sees in the world today?
5. In what ways are we responsible for it, and what should we do?
6. What do you think God was doing about the wickedness in the world when He sent Jesus?
7. Of what promise of God does the rainbow remind us? Can you think of other promises of His?
8. What is your part in helping His promises to come true?
9. Can you think of some promises you should make to God?

Chapter Two

A CHEATER'S DREAM

Suppose you did something that was very wrong, and you knew you should be punished. But instead of punishing you, your parents forgave you and told you how very special you were to them. How would you feel? Would you be so relieved and thankful that you would try to be a better person ever after?

If so, you will understand how Jacob felt after his wonderful dream. But that is not where the story begins.

★ ★ ★ ★ ★ ★ ★ ★

Jacob and Esau were twin brothers, but Esau was born first. In those days, that meant that one day he would get more of their father's property. This was called his "birth-right." As the boys grew up, Esau loved to be outdoors and became a good hunter. But Jacob liked to stay at home. He even learned to cook.

One afternoon, Jacob had a pot of meat and vegetables boiling when Esau came in from hunting. Esau was very tired and hungry. When he saw Jacob's stew, his mouth began

13

to water. He said, "That smells good. Give me some before I faint; I'm starving!"

Jacob saw his chance to get ahead of his brother: "You may have all you can eat, if you first sell me your birthright."

Esau thought, "What good will my birthright be to me if I die from hunger?" So he agreed to what Jacob said. How foolish he was to sell his birthright for one meal! But also, how selfish Jacob was!

Of course, Esau and Jacob did not tell their father Isaac about this agreement. So, years later, when Isaac was old and blind, one day he called for Esau and said, "My son, take your bow and arrows, go out into the field and find some fresh game. Then cook me a meal such as I like, and I will give you my blessing and your birthright."

But before Esau came back, Jacob killed two little goats from the flock, and, with his mother's help, he cooked the kind of meal that Isaac liked and carried it in to him, pretending that he was Esau. Isaac wondered how Esau could be back so soon. "Are you really my son, Esau?" he asked.

Jacob told an out-and-out lie. "Yes, I am," he said.

Then Isaac gave him the blessing that he thought he was giving to Esau. So, for a second time, Jacob cheated his brother. After that, Esau hated Jacob and said to himself, "One of these days, I will kill him."

Because of this, Jacob decided to leave and go to a distant country called Padan-Aram and live there with an uncle whose name was Laban.

Now we come to Jacob's first night away from home! He had no place to sleep except outdoors. So after the sun had set, he found himself a big smooth rock for a pillow and lay down under the stars. And as he slept, he had a dream.

What kind of dream do you suppose it was? A bad dream? A nightmare? That is surely the kind of dream he deserved because of the way he had treated his brother! But how thankful all of us should be that God treats us better than we deserve. That was the way God treated Jacob on his first night away from home—He came to him in a truly wonderful dream!

In that dream, Jacob saw a long ladder set up on the earth. The top of it reached all the way to Heaven, and angels were moving up and down on it. Above it, God was standing, and He said to Jacob, "I am the God of your grandfather Abraham and of your father Isaac, and I will be your God also. The land on which you are lying I will give to you and to your descendants (your children and your grandchildren). And through you and your descendants, I will bless all nations of the earth. I will be with you and keep you wherever you go, and I will bring you back to this

Jacob Dreams at Bethel

land. I will never leave you until I have done all that I have promised."

That was truly a wonderful dream—just the opposite of what Jacob deserved! No wonder when he woke up, he said, "Surely the Lord is in this place. This is none other than the house of God, and this is the gate of Haven." Then he named the place Bethel, which means, God's house. Before Jacob left to go on his way, he set up the stone on which he had slept as a monument and made a solemn promise to God: "Of all that You give me, I will give back one tenth to You."

Jacob was never the same after his dream at Bethel. Then and there he began to become a different and better man. Some twenty years later, God came to him again and said, "Your name shall not be Jacob any longer, but Israel."

Just how different he had become by that time you can judge for yourself when I tell you that his old name, Jacob, means Cheater, while the new name God gave him, Israel, means God's Prince.

Prayer

Dear God, many times You have treated me so much better than I deserve—just as You did Jacob. Make me truly thankful for how good You are to me, and help me to prove how thankful I am by being the kind of person you want me to be. In Jesus' name, amen.

★ ★ ★ ★ ★ ★ ★ ★

QUESTIONS ON CHAPTER TWO

1. Describe how Jacob cheated his brother Esau.
2. How do you feel when someone tricks you or cheats you?
3. Why did Jacob leave home?
4. Describe Jacob's dream and the promise God made to him.
5. What promises do you know of that God has promised you?
6. Why did Jacob name the place "Bethel"? What did the name mean?
7. What promise did Jacob make to God?
8. How do we know that Jacob later became a different and better man?
9. Do you think God is trying to make you a better person too? How?
10. What can you do to allow God to make you a better person?

Chapter Three

THE CHEATER'S FEAR

Which do you think is harder: to say, "I'm sorry," and ask someone to forgive you; or to say, "That's O.K.," and forgive and forget? Well, neither is easy, is it?

But how unhappy two people can be when one has done a wrong against the other and neither tries to make it right. And what a relief and joy both feel when they finally get together and make up. The Bible tells us about two brothers who did just that.

★ ★ ★ ★ ★ ★ ★ ★

The servant was trembling as he rushed into Jacob's tent. "My lord, your brother Esau is coming!" he said. "Look, on yonder hill, you can see him, and with him are four hundred men!" Then Jacob, too, was frightened! He remembered as though it were yesterday how he had cheated his brother twenty years earlier.

To get away from Esau's anger, Jacob had run away to the land of Padan-Aram. There he lived for twenty years with his uncle Laban. He married and became the father of twelve sons and one daughter. He also had

19

become quite wealthy in sheep and goats. Now, with all his possessions and his family, he was coming back, as God had commanded him, to the land where he was born.

No wonder he was afraid when he saw Esau coming with four hundred men! The wrong he had done to his brother twenty years earlier had never been set right. It was his guilty conscience that made him afraid. And Esau had said he would kill Jacob!

But though he was afraid, Jacob did a very wise thing. He turned to God in prayer and said, "O God, I am not worthy of even one of Your little blessings. Truly You have been good and kind to me. I had nothing but a staff in my hand when I left my home twenty years ago. Now, as I come back, I have a great flock of sheep and goats. You said to me, 'Come back to your country and to your people,' and You promised, 'I will deal well with you.' So save me now, I pray, and my family, from Esau, and let me find grace and forgiveness from him."

When he had finished praying, Jacob hurried to send not one, but five generous presents to Esau. He ordered his servants to take with them, drove by drove, with a space between each, 220 goats, 220 sheep, sixty camels, fifty cows, and thirty donkeys.

As each servant came to Esau, he bowed and said, as Jacob had told him to do, "These are from your brother Jacob, a present to

Jacob and Esau Meet Again

you, my lord. And he himself is coming to greet you."

When at last Jacob and his family came in sight, Esau ran to meet him, not in anger but in forgiveness. Esau threw his arms around Jacob, fell on his neck, and kissed him! As they wept upon each other's shoulder, Esau asked, "What do you mean by all these animals you sent?"

"They are a present for you, my brother, because I wanted you to forgive me."

"But I have enough," Esau answered, "and no present is needed, dear brother. Keep your flocks and herds for yourself. I have already forgiven you."

But Jacob insisted: "Then accept my present as an expression of my gratitude, my brother. You have been so very kind and forgiving that looking into your face is like seeing the face of God."

Wasn't that a wonderful thing for Jacob to say? And also how true! We too help others to see what God is like when we are forgiving and kind to those who have done wrong to us. So Esau and Jacob became true brothers again, thus showing to the world what a beautiful thing it is to forgive and forget!

Prayer
Dear God, if anyone has done a wrong against me, help me to forgive and to forget and to treat that person as if nothing had ever

come between us. And if I have done a wrong against someone else, give me the courage to say, "I'm sorry," and to ask to be forgiven.

May I always be kind to the members of my family and my friends, tenderhearted and forgiving as You have always been to me. In Jesus' name, amen.

★ ★ ★ ★ ★ ★ ★ ★

QUESTIONS ON CHAPTER THREE

1. Which is harder for you: (1) to apologize and ask to be forgiven or (2) to accept an apology and forgive?
2. What do you think of someone who says, "I forgive, but I can't forget"?
3. If we are not willing to forgive someone, what do you think we are asking for when we pray, "Forgive us our debts, as we forgive our debtors"?
4. Why was Jacob afraid of Esau? What did he do to win Esau's goodwill?
5. Can you think of anyone you should "go to meet" as Esau "went to meet" Jacob? Will you do it?

* For another beautiful story of forgiveness in your Bible, read Luke 15:11-24.

Chapter Four

DOWN WITH THE DREAMER!

How do you feel about dreams? Do they tell something about the future or not? There was a time when people thought a good dream meant something good was going to happen. A bad dream meant just the opposite.

Once there was a boy who dreamed that someday he would be great and famous. It was a long time before that dream came true, but it finally did! In the years before it came true, many things that were hard to take happened to that boy. But through them all, he kept his faith in God, and God made them work together for *good*.

God still has a way of bringing good out of bad for those who trust Him.

★ ★ ★ ★ ★ ★ ★ ★

Joseph was next to the youngest in a family of twelve brothers. His father, Jacob, loved Joseph more than the older brothers, and the older brothers didn't like Joseph at all.

One of the reasons Joseph's brothers hated

him was his dreams. One day Joseph said to his brothers, "Guess what I dreamed last night."

"We don't care. Keep your dreams to yourself!" they said.

Joseph told them anyway. "Last night," he said, "I dreamed that all of us were working together in the wheat field. The wheat was ripe, and we were cutting it and tying it into bundles. All of a sudden, my bundle stood straight up, and your bundles marched up and bowed down in front of mine."

"What a stupid dream!" they said. "Do you really think that someday you will be our master and we will be your servants?" And they laughed at him, calling him, "Your majesty, King Joseph!"

On another night, Joseph dreamed that the sun and moon and eleven stars bowed down in front of him. You would have thought Joseph would have kept that dream to himself. But he told it to his brothers, too, and they hated him more than ever. Then he told it to his father. And he didn't like it either.

"Joseph," he said, "you shouldn't talk like that! You are too proud. It's foolish for you to think that I and your mother and your brothers will ever bow down before you!" But still, his father wondered whether Joseph might become a mighty ruler someday.

Joseph's brothers hated him also because of his special coat. His father had given it to him as a present. His coat was the most beautiful coat they had ever seen. None of the brothers had ever received such a present; so they were both angry with their father and jealous of Joseph. "One of these days, we'll get even," they said. And sure enough, they did!

One morning soon after Joseph's seventeenth birthday, his father said to him, "Joseph, your brothers are over in the valley near the village of Shechem, taking care of the sheep. Take them this basket of food, find out how they are getting along, and then come back and tell me whether they are all right."

So Joseph started out toward Shechem, carrying the basket and wearing his beautiful coat. But when his brothers saw him coming, one said, "Look who's coming—that high and mighty brother of ours. He thinks he's so much better than we are! Let's throw him into a pit and leave him. That should put an end to his dreams!"

So, they grabbed Joseph, pulled off his new coat, and shoved him into a deep pit. Then they sat down and began eating the food that Joseph had brought them. Later, they looked up and saw a band of merchants with a train of camels coming toward them. The merchants were from the land of Midian and were on their way to Egypt to sell their spices and perfumes. This gave Joseph's brothers a new

Joseph's Brothers Prepare to Sell Him

idea. "Let's sell him to the merchants," one said.

"Great!" said another. "We'll be rid of him without killing him!"

"And get some money besides!" said a third.

So they pulled him up out of the pit and sold him to the merchants from Midian for twenty silver coins. But they kept his coat. As soon as the merchants were out of sight, they killed a goat, dipped the coat in the goat's blood, and took it back to their father.

"Look what we found!" they said. "This couldn't be Joseph's coat, could it?" Wasn't that a cruel thing to do!

Jacob recognized the coat and began to cry. "Yes, it is Joseph's coat," he sobbed. "I sent him to take you a basket of food. A lion or a bear must have killed him and dragged him away."

Jacob was so sad, thinking Joseph was dead, that he kept on weeping day after day. No one was able to comfort him.

"Joseph was so dear to me," he said. "As long as I live, I will be sad because he is gone!"

In the meantime, the merchants arrived in Egypt with Joseph. They sold him as a slave to an Egyptian army officer by the name of Potiphar. God was with Joseph, and Potiphar treated Joseph very kindly. He put him in charge of his whole household. Joseph knew

God was with him; so he was happy even though he was far from home.

★ ★ ★ ★ ★ ★ ★ ★

Prayer

Dear God, if I have more than some of my friends have, may I be grateful but not proud. If some of my friends have more than I have, may I be glad for them but not jealous. Make me happy with the things I have, ready to share, and never selfish, envious, or mean. In Jesus' name, amen.

★ ★ ★ ★ ★ ★ ★ ★

QUESTIONS ON CHAPTER FOUR

1. Why did Joseph's brothers hate him? Was this partly Joseph's fault?
2. Did Joseph talk too much about his dreams?
3. How would you have felt if you were one of Joseph's brothers? How would you have treated him?
4. Which do you think was worse—what Joseph's brothers did to him or what they did to their father?
5. What can you do about pride and jealousy in your life?
6. What is your "dream" for the future? Is it a "dream" God would approve of?

Chapter Five

JAILBIRD

I hope it will never happen to you, but how do you think you would feel if someone told a lie about you, and, because of that lie, you were thrown into prison? On top of that, suppose this happened to you when you were far from home in a strange country with no family or friends to help you. What would you do? Would you say to yourself, "It doesn't pay to be good anymore," and give up?

Well, all this happened to Joseph. Do you suppose he gave up?

★ ★ ★ ★ ★ ★ ★ ★

"Good morning, my friend," said Joseph. "Why do you look so sad today?" Joseph was speaking to one of his fellow prisoners. His name was Pashah.

"I am sad because of a strange dream I had last night," Pashah answered, "and because I cannot find anyone to tell me what it means."

"Maybe I can help you," said Joseph. "Dreams come from God. Tell me your dream, and I will pray to Him to reveal its meaning to us."

30

Now Pashah had once been chief butler to Pharaoh, the king of Egypt. Every day he had prepared the king's meals and served them to him in the palace. But one day he did something which Pharaoh did not like; so the king ordered him thrown into prison. There he and Joseph became good friends.

But why was Joseph in prison? Not because he had done something wrong, but because someone told a lie about him when he was a slave in the house of Potiphar. Potiphar was the Egyptian army officer who bought him from the Midianite merchants after he had been sold to them by his brothers. It was Potiphar's wife who told the lie. Since Joseph was only a slave, he was not given a trial. Potiphar simply threw him into prison.

But Joseph did not allow himself to become discouraged. He still trusted God. Also, he did everything he could to help and cheer up the other prisoners. Because of this, they all liked him, and before long the warden of the prison put him in charge of all the other prisoners.

But back to Pashah. This is the dream he told Joseph. "In my dream I was standing beside a vine which had three branches. Suddenly, buds appeared on the vine, then blossoms, then bunches of ripe grapes. I had Pharaoh's cup in my hand. I took the grapes, squeezed the juice into the cup and gave it to Pharaoh."

Pasha's Dream

After Joseph had prayed to God for wisdom, he turned to Pashah and said, "This is the meaning of your dream: the three branches of the vine stand for three days. In three days Pharaoh will send for you to come to the palace. You will be his butler again and will serve him food and wine as you used to do."

Then Pashah was no longer sad, but very happy. "Joseph, you are truly a wonderful friend," he said. "I wish there were something I could do to show you how grateful I am!"

"There *is* something you can do for me," said Joseph. "You remember, as I once told you, I was sold by my brothers and carried away from my home. Also, in my master Potiphar's house, I did nothing wrong that should cause him to put me into this prison. When you go back to the palace, tell the king about me and ask him to set me free."

Pashah promised, but when he was restored to his place in the palace, he was so busy with his duties and so lost in his own happiness that he forgot his promise. In fact, it was two whole years before he ever remembered Joseph. Pashah was not really very grateful, was he? Grateful people remember people who do kind things for them. Remember that the next time someone is kind to you.

Prayer

Dear God, help me not to give up when I feel blue. When I am discouraged, may I remember this is the time, above all other times, to be brave.

Teach me, too, that when I help others, as Joseph did, I make my own troubles much lighter. And help me to remember those who are kind to me so I can thank them. In Jesus' name, amen.

★ ★ ★ ★ ★ ★ ★ ★

QUESTIONS ON CHAPTER FIVE

1. What are some of the "wrong" things Joseph could have done while he was in prison?
2. What were the "right" things he did do?
3. What do you think would have happened to Joseph if he had been angry and mean as a prisoner?
4. If someone told a lie about you, or blamed you for something which was not your fault, what would you do?
5. How do you feel about people who break their promises to you?
6. Can you think of any promises you may have forgotten? (1) to God? (2) to a member of your family? (3) to a friend?
7. What should you do about the promises you have forgotten?

Chapter Six

FROM PRISON TO PALACE

What is the most wonderful surprise that ever happened to you? Was it a surprise that someone planned for you? Was it just luck? Or was it something God did for you? Was your surprise something for you alone, or were you able to share it with someone else?

★ ★ ★ ★ ★ ★ ★ ★

Pharaoh, the king of Egypt, got up early. He paced the floor of his room, deep in thought. He called together his wise men and talked with them for some time. Then they left, and the king was still pacing.

When Pashah, the king's butler, brought in Pharaoh's breakfast, he could tell the king was troubled. "Why is my lord so worried this morning?" he asked.

"I hardly slept at all last night," replied the king. "I had two strange dreams, and I have no idea what they mean. Already I have called in my wise men and magicians, but none of them can explain the dreams to me."

Then Pashah remembered a promise he had made two years earlier. He felt very sorry that he had not remembered sooner. He had promised to tell the king about Joseph, who was in prison for no good reason.

"My lord," he said, "when I was in prison, I had a dream that troubled me. Another prisoner was there, a wonderful young man named Joseph. I told him my dream, and he was able to tell me what it meant. Perhaps he could do the same for you."

"Send for him at once!" ordered Pharaoh.

When Joseph heard that the king had sent for him, he took time first to shave and bathe and put on fresh clothes. Then, looking his best, he hurried to the palace and stood before the king.

Pharaoh said to him, "Last night I had two dreams that have troubled me since. My butler tells me that you are able to explain the meaning of dreams. Is this true?"

"The power is not in me," Joseph replied, "but in God. Let the king tell his dreams to me, and God will give us the answer."

"In my first dream," Pharaoh said, "I was standing beside the Nile River. There came up out of the water seven cows fat and smooth, and they began to eat grass in the meadow. After them, out of the river came up seven other cows—thin and ugly. I have never seen such ugly cows in all my life—at least, not in Egypt! Then the seven thin cows ate up the seven fat ones. But afterward they were still as thin and ugly as they were before. The dream woke me up.

"After a while, I fell asleep and dreamed again. In my second dream, I saw seven ears of corn—large, full, and good—all growing on one stalk. On another stalk were seven lean ears—withered, thin, and small. While I was looking, the seven thin ears ate up the seven good ears. I have told these dreams to my wise men and magicians, but they were not able to explain their meaning."

Then Joseph said to the king: "God is telling Pharaoh what He is about to do. The two dreams mean one and the same thing. The seven fat cows and the seven large ears of corn stand for seven years of good crops and plenty of food that will come to the land of Egypt. After these will come seven years of hunger and famine, when the crops will fail and there will be great suffering.

"God is showing this to you so that you can prepare for the famine and save your people. Therefore, I urge the king to seek out and find a man who is both wise and good and make him governor over all the land of Egypt. Let this man have officers under him who will gather, during the seven years of plenty, large supplies of grain and put them in great storehouses in the cities. Then, when the years of famine come, there will be food to keep the people from starving."

Then Pharaoh said to his servants and court officers, "Where could we find anyone wiser and better than this man who has told

Joseph Interprets Pharaoh's Dream

us these things?'' Turning to Joseph, he said, ''Since the spirit of God is in you, and since He has made known all these things to you, you shall be governor over the land of Egypt and in charge of gathering and storing up the grain before the years of famine.''

Then the king took off his ring and put it on Joseph's finger, and he ordered that Joseph should be dressed in a gorgeous robe, with a chain of gold around his neck. Also he had him ride through the streets in a chariot behind his own, and all the people bowed before him. So God brought Joseph out of prison and made him governor over all the land of Egypt. All this was part of God's wonderful plan!

Seven years later, when the famine came, Joseph sold the grain that he had stored up during the seven years of plenty. Thus, he was able to save thousands of people from starving. Even his own family, including the brothers who had sold him into Egypt, might have starved but for Joseph and what he was able to do for them.

Prayer

Dear God, when something good happens to me, may I remember it is because You love me. May I be grateful but not proud. Then may I show my gratitude by doing things that will help others just as Joseph did. In Jesus' name, amen.

★ ★ ★ ★ ★ ★ ★ ★

QUESTIONS ON CHAPTER SIX

1. What do you think would have happened if Joseph had said, "I don't care how I look?" when he left the prison to go to meet Pharaoh?
2. How do we know Joseph did care how he looked? Did it pay?
3. How was Joseph able to explain dreams?
4. How does God help you in the things you are called upon to do?
5. Do you think everything you have is a gift from God? See 1 Corinthians 4:7. How should you treat these "gifts"?
6. Why did Pharaoh believe that Joseph would make a good governor? Should Christians make better workers and officials than people who are not Christians?
7. If Joseph were here today, what do you think he would do about the starving people in the world?
8. What should we do about it? What can you do about it?
9. Do you think it is wrong to eat too much or to waste food? Why?

Chapter Seven

FROM FEAST TO FAMINE

Isn't it amazing how some people are able to hide the bad things they do? They may cheat at school, steal from a store, rob a bank, or even kill someone, and they are never found out.

But there is a verse in the Bible that says, "Be sure your sin will find you out" (Numbers 32:23). That means that while we may be able to hide our sins from others, we cannot hide them from God or ourselves. When we do something wrong, the memory of it follows us like our shadow everywhere we go. Our conscience won't let us forget it, and we will always be troubled by it unless we do what we should to correct the wrong. And that was just the problem Joseph's brothers had.

Soon after Joseph was made governor of Egypt, Pharaoh's dream began to come true. All over the land, the fields brought forth big harvests. And Joseph, wise governor that he was, lost no time in buying up the grain and storing it in great barns which he had built in

41

the cities. For seven years, he did this. Then the seven years of famine began, and the people of Egypt came to buy back the grain they had sold to Joseph. The famine even reached other countries; so people came (to Egypt) from far away to buy grain.

One day in Canaan, where Joseph's father, Jacob, and his family still lived, Jacob said to his sons, "Why do you look so worried? Although our grain is almost gone, I have heard that there is plenty in Egypt. Saddle the donkeys; go down and buy some for us. If we do nothing, we will starve." So the ten oldest, each riding a donkey, set out for Egypt. But Benjamin, the youngest, stayed with Jacob.

Now Joseph and Benjamin were "full" brothers; they had the same mother. Her name was Rachel, but she was no longer living. The other ten were "half" brothers to Joseph and Benjamin. This explains why Joseph always felt closer to Benjamin than to any of his other brothers. It also explains why Jacob wanted Benjamin, his youngest son, to stay with him.

Some days later, Joseph's ten half-brothers arrived in Egypt, asked where they could buy grain, and were sent to the governor's office. Now when they sold Joseph as a slave some fifteen years earlier, they never dreamed he would one day become governor; so none of them recognized him. But Joseph did recognize them.

As they bowed before him with their faces to the ground, Joseph wondered whether they were still as selfish and cruel as they were on the day they threw him into the pit and sold him, or whether they had changed and were now good, kind, and honest. He decided to test them. So instead of telling them who he was and speaking kindly to them, he said in a stern voice, "You are spies! You have come to see what our country is like. Then you will go back and tell our enemies."

"No, my lord," they said. "We are not spies but honest men. Everything we have told you is the truth. We are brothers, all the sons of one man in the land of Canaan. We have come to Egypt for only one purpose. Our father Jacob sent us to buy grain because of the famine."

"Do you have any other brothers?" Joseph asked.

"Yes, two others," they answered. "One, whose name was Joseph, is dead; the youngest one, whose name is Benjamin, is with our father back in Canaan."

"You say you are telling the truth?" replied Joseph, "and you have a younger brother? You must prove it! One of you may go back and carry food to your home. The rest of you will stay here as my prisoners. You will be set free only if your youngest brother is brought to Egypt. I must see him

with my own eyes! Then I will believe you."
Then he put them all in prison for three days.

On the third day, Joseph pretended to have
changed his mind. "I will keep only one of
you," he said. "The rest may return to your
homes with food. But you must bring your
youngest brother back with you to prove you
are not lying."

At this point, Joseph's brothers turned and
began talking with one another in Hebrew,
thinking Joseph could not understand what
they were saying. They thought he was an
Egyptian because he had used an interpreter
(a man who spoke both Hebrew and Egyptian) to talk to them. But Joseph heard and
understood every word.

"All this has happened because of what we
did to our brother Joseph years ago," said
one.

"Our sin has found us out," another
added.

"I remember how he cried, stretched out
his hands, and begged us not to sell him," a
third said.

"Yes," said Reuben, the oldest, "and I
pleaded with you not to harm him, but you
wouldn't listen. Now God is punishing us!"

As Joseph listened, he couldn't keep back
his tears. He walked out of the room so his
brothers wouldn't see him crying. He saw
they were changing, and so great was his love
for them that he wanted to forgive them then

Joseph Sends His Brothers Away

and there. But he decided it was best to go ahead with the test.

So he came back and ordered Simeon, the second oldest, to be put in prison. "He will be set free," said Joseph, "only if you prove you have told me the truth by bringing your youngest brother to Egypt. Unless you bring him, I will not sell you any more grain."

So the other brothers loaded their sacks, which Joseph's servants had filled with grain, on their donkeys and started back to Canaan.

When they stopped for the first night, they made an amazing discovery. They opened their sacks and found that every man's bag of money was in the top of his sack!

When they saw this, they were amazed and also afraid. Of course, none of them knew Joseph had ordered his servants to put the money there as they filled the sacks.

When they arrived home, they told their father all that had happened in Egypt—how the governor had accused them of being spies and telling lies and had said he would not sell them any more grain or set their brother Simeon free unless they brought Benjamin down with them.

They did not know that all of this would have a happy ending. But they had learned how wicked they had been in selling Joseph as a slave. They were now beginning to listen to their conscience—and all of this points to a happy ending.

Prayer

Dear God, when I do something that makes me feel bad inside, may I know that it is because my conscience is telling me what I did was wrong. Then help me to do what my conscience tells me I should do to set the wrong right so I may feel right inside again. In Jesus' name, amen.

QUESTIONS ON CHAPTER SEVEN

1. How did Joseph prepare for the famine?
2. Why did Joseph feel closer to Benjamin than to the other brothers?
3. If your brothers had treated you as Joseph's brothers did him, how would you feel if they came to you for help? What would you do?
4. How did Joseph feel about his brothers when they came to him? What did he wonder about them?
5. How did Joseph test his brothers?
6. Do you think Joseph was fair to them? Why or why not?
7. When you have done something wrong, how do you feel inside?
8. What should you do to set the wrong right?
9. When should you do it?

Chapter Eight

DINNER IN THE PALACE

Suppose you had had a bad day at school—someone shoved you as you were coming down the steps, or someone said something ugly about you or laughed at you when you made a mistake. How would you feel about going back the next day?

You wouldn't want to go, would you? You would be tempted to say you had a headache and stay home. But deep down you would know that you had to go back. You couldn't get an education if you stayed away. So, even though you would dread it, you would go back. And later you would be glad you did.

★ ★ ★ ★ ★ ★ ★

It was time for Jacob's sons to go back to Egypt for more grain, but they didn't want to go. They were afraid because of the way they had been treated the first time. They wondered what the governor would say about the money they had found in their sacks. They wondered if their brother Simeon, whom the governor had put in prison, was still alive. These were some of the reasons they didn't want to go back.

But their supply of grain was almost gone and famine was still everywhere. Only in Egypt could they buy grain. So one morning Jacob said to his sons, "You will have to go back to Egypt and buy us some more grain."

"Then we will have to take Benjamin with us," said Judah.

"No. He is my youngest son. I have told you before; he will stay with me. I cannot do without him," Jacob replied.

"Then there is no use for us to go," Judah said. "The governor told us over and over that he would not even see us unless we brought Benjamin with us."

"But why did you tell him you had another brother?" said Jacob.

"He asked us all about our family," Judah answered. " 'Is your father still alive? Do you have another brother?' were his very words. We had no way of knowing that he would say, 'You must bring your youngest brother with you the next time you come.' But he really meant it. That's the reason he would not let Simeon come back with us."

"Oh, what shall I do?" said Jacob. "Joseph is dead. And Simeon may be dead, too. I cannot bear to lose Benjamin, my youngest son."

Judah laid his hand on his father's shoulder and said, "Listen, Father. Put him in my care. I give you my solemn promise that I will see that no harm comes to him and will bring him back. But we must have food. Let us go before we starve."

So Jacob gave in. "I suppose there's nothing else to do," he said, "but take a present of fruit and honey and nuts to the governor, and also extra money so you can return what was found in your bags. And may God give the governor a tender heart, that he may set Simeon free and send Benjamin back."

So Jacob's sons set out again for the land of Egypt. A few days later, they arrived at the governor's office. When Joseph was told that they were there and that their youngest brother was with them, he said to his chief officer, "Invite them to my palace and prepare your best dinner for them."

But when Judah and his brothers heard they were to have dinner at the governor's palace, they were afraid and said to one another. "It is because of the money we found in our sacks. The governor is going to throw us into prison with Simeon."

So they told the governor's chief officer about the money and offered to give it back. But he would not take it. "You don't owe anything," he said. "I myself remember you paid your bill in full when you were here before. God must have put the money in your sacks."

Then he brought out Simeon and took them all to the governor's palace. Soon the governor came in, and Reuben stepped forward, bowed, and offered the presents of fruit and honey and nuts they had brought. As he did, his brothers all fell to their knees before the governor. Joseph thanked them, then asked, "How is your father, the old man about whom you told me before?"

"Our father is still alive and is well," they answered.

Then, seeing Benjamin, his youngest brother whom he loved so dearly, Joseph said, "And this, I take it, is your youngest brother you told me about?" Turning to Benjamin he added, "May God bless you, my son."

At this point, Joseph hurriedly left the room. So great was the love he felt for Benjamin that he could not keep from crying. As soon as he had dried his tears and washed his face, he came back. "Let dinner be served," he said to his servants, and he led his brothers to the table. They were amazed to find their places had been arranged in the order of their ages—the oldest first, and so on down to the youngest. They could not understand how the governor knew their ages! But they did know it was very special to be having dinner in his palace. So, as they sat at the table eating and drinking, they forgot their fears and had a good time together.

★ ★ ★ ★ ★ ★ ★ ★

Prayer

Dear God, keep me from expecting life to

51

Joseph's Brothers Eat Dinner at the Palace

be always pleasant. Every day I am called upon to do things that I don't like to do. But help me to do them anyway even when it is hard, when I know I should! May I do what is right, just because it is right. In Jesus' name, amen.

★ ★ ★ ★ ★ ★ ★ ★

QUESTIONS ON CHAPTER EIGHT

1. Why didn't Jacob's sons want to go back to Egypt?
2. Why did they have to go? Why did Benjamin have to go?
3. How did Jacob feel about letting Benjamin go?
4. How do you think Benjamin felt about going to Egypt?
5. Could you make someone a promise like the one Judah made to his father? Why might you do it?
6. Why did Joseph leave the room after he had greeted Benjamin? How do you suppose his brothers felt? What might they guess as possible reasons for his leaving?
7. What does the word "duty" mean to you?
8. Do you have any duties? What are they?
9. How should you perform them? Do you? Will you?

Chapter Nine

MISSING—THE
GOVERNOR'S CUP!

Suppose you felt very sad inside because of some wrong you had done to some member of your family or dear friend. You knew you were guilty and had not been forgiven. You'd feel pretty bad, wouldn't you?

Then suppose all of a sudden, all that changed! You said you were sorry and you were forgiven. Wouldn't that be a wonderful feeling?

★ ★ ★ ★ ★ ★ ★ ★

On the night Joseph had his brothers for dinner in his house, he watched how they acted toward each other and was almost sure they were now kind and good and no longer mean and cruel as they had been when they sold him into Egypt. But the next morning he decided to put them to one more test.

Calling to his chief officer, he said, "Fill their bags with grain, and again, put every man's money in the mouth of his bag and tie it tight. But in the top of the bag of the youngest also put my *silver cup!*"

The officer did as he was told, and soon after, Joseph's brothers rode away, each with a bag of grain. They had gone only a little way when Joseph said to his officer: "Hurry! Go after the men, ask them why they have given evil for good by stealing my silver cup."

The officer soon caught up with them and ordered them to stop. "You are thieves," he said. "The governor was so good to you, and you have stolen his silver cup!"

"We are not thieves, but honest men," they answered. "Don't you remember how we brought back the money we found in our bags when we bought the grain before? We have stolen nothing. Search our bags, and if you find the cup, all of us will become your master's slaves."

Quickly each opened his bag, beginning with the oldest, and the youngest last. In each man's bag was his money, and Joseph's silver cup was found in Benjamin's bag!

The brothers hurried back to Joseph's office. They bowed before him, terribly afraid. Then Judah said, "My lord, we don't know what to say. We are ready to become your slaves, both we and our youngest brother in whose bag your cup was found."

"No," said Joseph. "Only he shall be my slave. The rest of you go on home!"

Then Judah, remembering his promise to his father, came close to Joseph and said, "O my lord, our father is an old man. Benjamin

A Soldier Finds Joseph's Cup

is his youngest son, and he loves him very dearly. If we go back without him, he will die. My lord, before we left to come back to Egypt, I promised my father that I would see that no harm came to Benjamin and that I would surely bring him back. So, I plead with you, let me stay as your slave, my lord, but let the boy go back with his brothers, so that our father's heart may not be broken.''

At this point Joseph could keep his secret no longer. He dismissed his servants, then broke down and cried. He said, ''I am Joseph your brother. Do not be afraid. I have only been testing you. And I know that you are now kind and good men and loyal to each other. I have forgiven you, and God has made everything turn out for good. He has made me governor over all the land of Egypt, and through me has saved your lives and the lives of many others during this time of famine.''

Then Joseph took Benjamin into his arms, and they laughed and cried as they hugged one another. He kissed all his brothers, and they laughed and cried too—both for sorrow and for joy!

Prayer

Dear God, how I hate that bad feeling inside of me when I have done something wrong. I do thank you that there is a way to get rid of that feeling. Whenever I do or say something I shouldn't to a friend or a member of my family, may I say, "I'm sorry," and ask to be forgiven. Help me to show my love for my family and my friends by being always loyal and doing everything I can to make them happy. In Jesus' name, amen.

★ ★ ★ ★ ★ ★ ★ ★

QUESTIONS ON CHAPTER NINE

1. Why did Joseph "test" his brothers? How did he test them?
2. Do you feel different about Joseph's brothers after Joseph's tests than you did when they sold him? Why or why not?
3. Why do you think Joseph ordered his silver cup to be put in Benjamin's sack instead of in the sack of one of the older brothers?
4. Why did Judah offer to save Benjamin?
5. Why did God allow Joseph to be sold into Egypt? Do you feel God also has a purpose in things that happen to you? (See Romans 8:28.)
6. How did Joseph prove he still loved his brothers?
7. What does it mean to you to be loyal . . .
   (1) To the members of your family?
   (2) To your friends?
   (3) To Jesus?
8. How did Jesus prove His loyalty to you? (See John 15:13.)

Chapter Ten

FAMILY REUNION

When we are young, perhaps we think too much about what we want our parents to do for us, and not enough about what we can and should do for them. Sometimes we may even feel a little ashamed because they do not dress as well or make as much money or have as good an education as the parents of some of our friends.

In Joseph's days, Egyptians thought shepherds were not as good as other people. But far from being ashamed of his shepherd-father, Joseph did something that showed he not only loved him, but was proud of him, too.

★ ★ ★ ★ ★ ★ ★ ★

When Joseph had finished telling his brothers who he was and that they had nothing to fear because he had forgiven them, he said, "And how is my father? Is he still alive and well?"

"He is alive and well," they answered, "but he is now an old man and growing feeble."

"You must hurry back to him and tell him

that God has made me governor over all the land of Egypt," said Joseph. "You must bring him down to be near me so I can take care of him, for there will still be five more years of the famine. You, too, must move to Egypt, my dear brothers," Joseph continued. "Bring your wives and children and all your possessions. Here you may care for your flocks and herds. I will look after you, and you will be safe from all fear of the famine."

So Joseph's brothers left with food and wagons to bring their families to Egypt. Not many days later, they arrived back home. Running to their father's tent, they shouted, "Joseph is still alive! He is governor over all the land of Egypt!" At first Jacob could not believe them. He almost fainted. The news was just too good to be true. But when they told him all the words Joseph had spoken and showed him the wagons and the food he had sent, joy came over the old man's face, and he said, "Say no more; I believe you! Joseph, my son, must be living; I will go to see him while I am still alive." So Jacob told his sons to fold their tents, pack their belongings and gather their flocks and herds. A few days later, they were on their way to Egypt.

When they arrived, Joseph went to the palace and said to Pharaoh: "My father and my brothers with their families are here. They have brought their flocks and their herds with them, for they are shepherds."

60

Then Pharaoh said: "The country of Egypt is before you. Settle them on the best of the land. Let them dwell in the land of Goshen. And put some of the men in charge of my cattle."

Now, of course, Joseph knew how the Egyptians felt about shepherds. They thought shepherds were not as good as everyone else. Still he was proud of his father and took him to the palace and introduced him to Pharaoh.

Pharaoh spoke kindly to him, then asked, "How old are you?"

"One hundred and thirty years," Jacob replied, "and my life has been full of trouble, because for so long I thought my son Joseph was dead."

"But now you see he is very much alive, and governor over all the land, second only to me!" Pharaoh replied. Then he added: "You and your sons are welcome. I have ordered the governor to allow you to settle in the best part of Egypt. The land of Goshen will be your home. There your sons will find good pastures for their flocks and herds and no danger of famine."

"The king is most kind," said Jacob. Then, as he and Joseph started to leave, he asked God to bless Pharaoh.

Thus it came about that Jacob was united again with his long-lost son. For many years, he and his other sons with their families lived happily together in the land of Egypt under

Jacob Meets Pharaoh

the loving care of Joseph, who continued to be the governor, second to the king only.

★ ★ ★ ★ ★ ★ ★ ★

Prayer

Dear God, help me to be as unselfish and forgiving, and as kind and helpful to all members of my family, as Joseph was to his brothers and his father. In Jesus' name, amen.

★ ★ ★ ★ ★ ★ ★ ★

QUESTIONS ON CHAPTER TEN

1. Why do you think Pharaoh was glad when he heard that Joseph's brothers were in Egypt? What did he say?
2. What message did Joseph send to his father?
3. What finally convinced Jacob that Joseph was still alive?
4. If you had been Joseph, would you have introduced your father to Pharaoh? Why or why not?
5. What were some of the things that made Jacob and his sons happy as they continued to live in the land of Egypt? Do you think they might have been homesick for Canaan sometimes? Why or why not?
6. Name ways you can be helpful to older people.
7. What does the Bible teach about how you should treat your father and mother? (See Ephesians 6:1, 2.)

Chapter Eleven

CRADLE IN THE RIVER

When you were a little baby, how many hours every day do you suppose your mother spent taking care of you? And did anyone pay her to do it? Of course not! She did it just because she loved you! But did you know there is a story in the Bible about a mother who really did get paid for taking care of her own baby? Her name was Jochebed.

Four hundred years had passed since Jacob and his sons with their families had moved to Egypt. Since that time, other kings, called pharaohs, had come to the throne. They did not remember Joseph and the promise the king had made about providing for his relatives. And all of Jacob's descendants, called Hebrews, or the people of Israel, had been made slaves.

★ ★ ★ ★ ★ ★ ★ ★

"Miriam," said Jochebed, "you have been so good to help me take care of your baby brother ever since he was born, but now he is three months old, and I am afraid we can't keep him in the house any longer."

Miriam was confused. "What do you mean,

Mother?'' she asked. "Isn't he safe here with us?''

"No, my dear, he is not safe. Pharaoh, the king, has given an order that every Hebrew baby shall be thrown into the river. Every day I am afraid his soldiers may come and search our house. You see, Miriam,'' she went on to explain, ''Pharaoh is afraid that if our boys should live and grow up, they will become strong and brave men who will fight and win freedom for our people. That is the reason he has ordered all Hebrew boy babies to be drowned.''

"Oh, Mother, what are we going to do?''

"I have a plan,'' said Jochebed, "and I need you to help me.''

Then she sent Miriam down to the river to gather and bring back an armful of the tall reeds which grew along the bank. Together they wove the reeds into a basket about the size and shape of a baby's cradle. Next they lined and sealed it with tar and pitch. When it was finished and dried, what do you suppose they had? A cradle that was also a boat!

The next morning, they put the baby into the little boat and hid him in the tall grass beside the river. Miriam stayed nearby to watch, so no harm could come to her little brother, while her mother went back to her duties in the house.

Before long, Miriam saw the Egyptian princess, with her maidens, coming down to the river to bathe! What should she do? Should she run and call her mother? If she did, the princess and her maidens might find the baby and carry him away before they could get back. They might even throw him into the river, as the king had ordered! So she stayed.

As she waited, she hoped the princess and her maidens wouldn't see the little boat hidden in the reeds. But they did! Soon, they were very close! The princess stopped and, pointing toward it, asked one of her maidens to bring it to her.

Then Miriam ran as fast as her feet could carry her down the path toward them. By the time she arrived, the princess had the basket in her hands. "What a darling baby!" she said. "This must be one of the Hebrew children." Her maidens said nothing, waiting to see what the princess would do. You see, she was the daughter of the king who had given the cruel order. Miriam waited, too. Then the baby began to cry! His tears came just at the right time. They touched the heart of the princess, and she took him out of the basket and held him in her arms!

"You dear little baby!" she said. "Shh, shh, don't you cry! No one is ever going to harm you. I am going to take you to the palace to be my own son. And your name will be Moses because we found you in the river" (*Moses* means "drawn out of the water").

A Maid Brings Moses to the Princess

Then Miriam came up to the princess. Bowing low, she said, "Would it please the princess if I find her a nurse to care for the baby?"

"Yes, my dear," replied the princess, "I shall most certainly need a nurse."

"My mother is the best nurse in the world!" said Miriam. "If you can wait for just a little, I will bring her."

Then up the path she ran, straight to her home. "Mother, Mother," she shouted as she pushed open the door. "Come right away! The princess sent me to bring you."

As they hurried down to the river, she told her mother the whole story. When the princess saw Jochebed, she was very pleased. "I found this baby in the reeds by the river bank in this little basket," she said. "Would you be willing to be his nurse? I will pay you well."

"But I could not leave my family," said Jochebed.

The princess agreed to let Jochebed keep Moses in her own home until he was older. Later he was brought to the palace and treated as if he were the son of the princess. There he went to the royal school, received a wonderful education, and became a very great man. But great and famous though he became, Moses never forgot his wonderful mother and his brave sister and how they had saved his life when he was a baby.

The Bible doesn't tell us how much the princess paid Jochebed for taking care of her own baby. But we can be sure that no amount of money could compare with the joy that was hers as she watched her little son growing up and in time becoming such a noble man. That has always been, and still is, a good mother's greatest reward!

Prayer

Dear God, I thank you for those who took care of me so lovingly when I was too little to take care of myself and for the way they still love me. May I never disappoint those who have done so much for me, who believe the best about me, and expect the best from me. In Jesus' name, amen.

★ ★ ★ ★ ★ ★ ★ ★

QUESTIONS ON CHAPTER ELEVEN

1. Why was Jochebed's baby not safe at home?
2. Why do you think Jochebed was a good mother?
3. What reasons can you find for liking Miriam?
4. How can you and your mother or father get along with each other and work together as well as Miriam and Jochebed did?
5. In what ways can you thank your parents for what they do for you?

Chapter Twelve

MYSTERY IN THE DESERT

Let us suppose that you were very rich. Imagine, too, that you owned a factory not far from your home. All the people in the factory had to work very hard and for long hours, but for very low wages; so they were very poor. Suppose one thing more—that among the pitiful people working in the factory were your father and mother and certain other members of your family.

Knowing all this, how would you feel? Would you be content to go on living for yourself in your beautiful home, thinking only of your own happiness? Or would you be very unhappy, troubled about your mother and father and the other people in the factory? Would you want to do something that would change things? What do you feel God would want you to do?

Your answer to these questions should help you to understand how Moses felt.

★ ★ ★ ★ ★ ★ ★ ★

When Moses became a man, he was not happy as a prince. His own people, the Hebrews, were slaves to the Egyptians!

He was both sad and angry as he saw what their cruel masters did to them and how much they suffered. The slaves had to make bricks out of mud and straw, and were often beaten because they did not make them fast enough. One day, Moses saw an Egyptian beating a Hebrew with a club. The Hebrew probably would have been killed; so Moses rushed to his rescue and killed the Egyptian.

The next day, Moses tried to break up a fight between two Hebrews. But one of them, the one who had started the fight, said, "Who made you our judge? Are you going to kill me as you killed the Egyptian yesterday?" When Moses heard that, he was afraid. He had hoped no one would find out about the Egyptian. But soon even Pharaoh knew it. Pharaoh ordered his police to find Moses and kill him.

Moses was afraid to stay in Egypt; so he went away to a land called Midian. There he sat down by a well. Soon seven sisters came to water their father's sheep, but some shepherds also came and tried to drive the women away so they could water their own sheep first. Again, Moses came to the rescue. Then he watered the sisters' sheep himself. The women were grateful and told their father, Jethro, about Moses. Jethro invited Moses to live with them. Moses even married one of Jethro's daughters.

One day, as Moses was watching after

Jethro's sheep in a desert place close to a mountain called Horeb, he saw a very strange sight. A bush was on fire, but it did not burn up! It just kept on burning!

Moses said to himself: "I will go up closer to see this strange sight, a bush on fire but not burning up!" As he came closer, he heard a voice. God was calling to him out of the bush.

The voice said, "Moses, I have seen the suffering of my people in the land of Egypt and have heard their cry because their masters are so cruel. I am going to deliver them from their slavery and bring them into a good new land, where they may live in freedom and worship and serve me as I shall command them."

Then the voice spoke again: "Moses, I have chosen *you* to deliver my people. I am going to send you to Pharaoh. You will tell him he must set my people free. Then you will lead them out of the land of Egypt and bring them into the new land which I will give them."

Then Moses said, "But I can't go to Pharaoh! He will not listen to me."

"I will be with you to help you and give you courage," God answered. "And I will give you power to work great signs and wonders until Pharaoh will let the people go. Then you will come and worship me upon this mountain."

"What if the Israelites say, 'Who sent

God Calls Moses from the Burning Bush

you?' " Moses asked. "When I say, 'The God of your fathers has sent me,' what if they say, 'What is His name?' What will I tell them?"

"I am who I am," God answered. "Tell them that 'I AM' sent you. Tell them I am the God of Abraham, Isaac, and Jacob."

"But what if they don't believe me?" Moses argued.

God answered: "What's that in your hand, Moses?"

"What, this?" said Moses. "Well, it's my rod."

"Throw it down."

When Moses threw it down, it became a snake, and Moses ran from it. But the Lord called him back. "Now pick it up—by the tail." Moses reached for the snake. It turned and looked at him; then it began to hiss. Moses was getting nervous, but he obeyed. As soon as he took hold of the snake, it became a rod again. God gave Moses power to work other signs, too.

Still Moses made excuses. "But I can't speak well," he said. "I would not know what to say to the king."

But God said, "Who made your mouth, Moses? I did. And I can put words in it for you. Now, go. I am with you to help you."

Still Moses held back. "O my Lord," he said. "I just can't. Please send someone else."

Then the Lord became angry. "Take Aaron your brother with you," He said. "He's a good speaker. I will tell him what to say, also. Together you will go to Pharaoh and tell him to set my people free. At first he will say no. But because of the miracles I will work through you, he will change his mind."

So, with God guiding and helping him, Moses went back to the land of Egypt. There he did become the great leader of his people. Later, they did come to Mt. Horeb, sometimes called Sinai, to the very place where God had called Moses. There they camped for several weeks to worship God and to thank Him for their new freedom. And there Moses received God's law, known today as the ten commands, to help God's people to live for Him.

Prayer

Dear God, I want my life to count someday for something fine and good. I believe You will help me, even as You helped Moses. Thank You for the Bible, which teaches me how to live for You and make my life count. As Moses did, may I listen and obey. In Jesus' name, amen.

★ ★ ★ ★ ★ ★ ★ ★

QUESTIONS ON CHAPTER TWELVE

1. Why was Moses not happy as a prince in Pharaoh's palace?

2. How do you feel when you are around

friends who don't have as many "nice things" as you do?

3. Do you ever feel bad about children who don't even have enough to eat? Is there anything you can do for them?
4. Why did Moses leave Egypt?
5. What work did he find to do in Midian?
6. What strange sight did he see in the desert one day?
7. What did God want Moses to do?
8. What do you think of the idea, "It is *my* life. I have the right to do what I want to do with it"?
9. How can you find out what God wants you to do with your life?
10. How many of the ten commandments do you know? Recite as many as you can.

Chapter Thirteen

GIANTS AND GRASSHOPPERS

Suppose for some good reason you needed to go through a dark forest at night. Suppose it was cloudy, so you couldn't see the moon or even the stars. Would you be afraid? Would you say, "I can't do it"?

Then suppose your father were to say, "I'll go with you"; would you still be afraid? Would you still say, "I can't do it"? That would not be the right answer, would it? It would mean that you were a coward.

There was a time that God's people were like that. They were cowards at heart and listened to the voice of fear, rather than to the voice of faith.

★ ★ ★ ★ ★ ★ ★ ★

The people of Israel were almost to Canaan, the land God had promised them in Egypt. You will remember they were led out of Egypt toward this new land by God's brave servant, Moses, and his brother, Aaron. For over a year, they had been moving toward it through a wild desert country where food was scarce and life was hard. But now, at last, they were close to Canaan.

Before they went on in, God told Moses to send men to spy out the land to see what it was like. Moses chose twelve men to do this. They were called spies or scouts.

As they set out, Moses said to them: "Go and see what the land is like, whether it is rich or poor, whether it is hilly or flat, and whether there are trees. Also see what the people are like. See whether they are strong or weak, few or many, and see where they live, whether in tents or in walled cities. Bring back some of the fruit of the land, too, that we may taste it. Be brave and bring back a true report."

The twelve scouts set out as Moses had commanded. They passed by a city called Hebron, where they saw men who were very tall and strong. Also they went through fertile valleys in which the vines were loaded with ripe grapes. They cut one big bunch of grapes and brought it back with them. It was so large that two men carried it between them on a long pole resting on their shoulders. They brought back some pomegranates and figs, too.

Forty days later, the scouts were back, and Moses and all the people came together to hear what they had to say. Now, of course, all twelve scouts had seen exactly the same things—the people, their number and size,

The Spies Return with Fruit from Canaan

their cities, their houses, their fields, and their vineyards. The only difference was that two, Joshua and Caleb, were men of courage and faith. The other ten were not.

The ten said: "The land is rich and fruitful. There is plenty of milk and honey. But the cities are like forts and the people are too strong; they are like giants. Compared to them, we are like grasshoppers. We cannot take the land."

But Joshua and Caleb said: "Do not lose faith in God or be afraid. If God is pleased with us, He will bring us into the land and will help us to take it."

The sad part of the story is that the people listened to the ten. They grumbled and complained against Moses and Aaron: "It would have been better if we had stayed in the land of Egypt," they said. "Why did you bring us out here in this desert where we may be killed by those giants in Canaan?"

So the people would not go up to take the land, and in the end they paid a big price for being cowards and complainers. For thirty-nine more years God let them wander in the desert country. There they suffered many more hardships and trials before He finally gave them the land as He had promised.

By that time, only two of the twelve scouts were still living. Can you guess which two they were? Yes, Joshua and Caleb, the two brave ones! That was the way God rewarded them for their courage—He kept them strong and well so they were able to march into Canaan and help His people conquer the land. Best of all, after Moses died, Joshua was chosen by God to be the brave captain who led the people in!

★ ★ ★ ★ ★ ★ ★ ★

Prayer
Dear God, I don't ever want to be a coward. But sometimes I feel alone and am afraid. When this happens, help me to remember that You are always with me and will give me courage. In Jesus' name, amen.

★ ★ ★ ★ ★ ★ ★ ★

QUESTIONS ON CHAPTER THIRTEEN
1. Why did Moses send scouts into Canaan?
2. What two reports did the scouts bring back?
3. Why were the reports different?
4. Which report did the people believe?
5. What do you think of the saying, "The majority is always right"?
6. Can you be a leader for things that are good if you always follow the crowd? How hard do you think it was for Joshua and Caleb to give their report with the other ten spies saying the opposite?
7. What are some of your fears? What do you do about them? How can God help you with them?

Chapter Fourteen

WANTED: A LEADER!

When something goes wrong in the world, what does God do about it? Does He set it right by His own mighty power? Sometimes, perhaps. But more often He finds and calls some brave person to help Him set the wrong right. That explains why Gideon became so well known in his day—and ours.

★ ★ ★ ★ ★ ★ ★ ★

Long after both Moses and Joshua were dead and God's people had settled in Canaan, their new land, they began to forget about God and to worship idols. Because of this, God allowed their enemies to attack them so they would repent.

One such enemy was the nation of Midian. The land of the Midianites was east of the Jordan River, but every year for seven years, they would cross over the river in great numbers at harvest time and steal the grain and sheep from the people of Israel. They would burn houses, take everything they could find, and leave no food at all, except the little the Israelites were able to hide in dens and caves back in the hills.

The people of Israel finally cried to God for help. And God answered them. He sent them a prophet who said: "This has happened because you have been worshiping the idols of the nations God drove out before you. You have forgotten the true God. You have not listened to His voice and have not obeyed His commandments."

The next thing God did in answer to their prayers was to call a young man by the name of Gideon to be their leader and deliverer.

One day, while Gideon was busy threshing his father's wheat, he kept wondering where he could hide it and why God allowed the Midianites to come into the land of Israel year after year. Did He no longer care about His people? Suddenly he looked up and saw an angel standing in front of him. "The Lord is with you," the angel said.

"If the Lord is with us," Gideon answered, "why has He allowed all of these things to happen to us? Where are His wonderful deeds about which our fathers told us when He brought them up out of their slavery in the land of Egypt? Has He now forgotten us?"

"God has not forgotten His people," the angel answered, "but they have sinned against Him by turning from Him and worshiping idols. If they will only turn back to Him, the true God, and serve Him, He will deliver them from the Midianites."

"But how will He do it?" asked Gideon.

"By you," the angel answered. "You are the man God will use to save His people from the Midianites. But before He does it, they must stop worshiping idols."

Now, not far from Gideon's home was a town in which an altar to a false god, known as Baal, was built. This altar, God said to Gideon, had to be destroyed. So that very night, Gideon with ten of his servants slipped into the town and tore down the altar to Baal. Then, upon the very same spot, they built an altar to the true God and put an offering on it.

Early the next morning, when the men of the city went out, as they did every day, to worship at the altar of Baal, it was gone! In its place was the new altar to the true God and on it the sacrifice Gideon had brought. The men were very angry and asked, "Who has done this?"

When they found out it was Gideon, they said to Joash, his father, "Bring out your son. He must die because he has torn down the altar of Baal."

But Joash answered, "Are you speaking up for Baal? If he is a god, let him speak up for himself! If he is not able to save his own altar, what kind of god is he?"

Thus, God's people were led to see how foolish they had been to worship Baal instead of the true God, who had led them out of the land of Egypt into the Land of Promise. After this, Gideon blew a trumpet and sent mes-

Gideon Destroys Baal's Altar

sengers all over the land to call men to come and help him fight the Midianites.

★ ★ ★ ★ ★ ★ ★ ★

Prayer

Dear God, I know your commandments are wise and good. They tell me what is right and what is wrong. They teach me what I should do and what I should not do. Help me to obey them, and please forgive me when I fail. In Jesus' name, amen.

★ ★ ★ ★ ★ ★ ★ ★

QUESTIONS ON CHAPTER FOURTEEN

1. What wicked things did the Midianites do to the people of Israel? Why did God allow these things to happen?

2. How did God plan to deliver His people from the Midianites?

3. What did the angel tell Gideon God's people must do before God would deliver them?

4. What brave thing did Gideon do to teach the people not to worship idols?

5. If an "idol" is anything we make more important than God, what "idols" give you trouble? How can you tear down these "idols"?

6. Do you see "idols" that other people "worship" today? How can you lead them to change?

7. Would you have the courage to risk your life to lead others to worship God?

Chapter Fifteen

SELECTING THE BRAVEST

Suppose you were in charge of an important and very dangerous job and needed three hundred brave men to help you get the job done. So you sent out far and wide by means of TV, radio, and newspaper a "Men Wanted" appeal.

Then, suppose several thousand men came. How would you go about selecting the three hundred needed? What tests would you use to make sure that the three hundred finally chosen were the bravest and the best?

Gideon had this very problem, and God gave him a special way to solve it.

★ ★ ★ ★ ★ ★ ★ ★

Gideon never thought of himself as a national leader. He was a farmer working with his father. But one day, an angel came to Gideon and said, "You are the man God will use to deliver His people from the Midianites." God had been using the Midianites to punish His people for their sins. But now God's people had repented and turned to God. So Gideon sent messengers throughout the land, calling for men to come and join his army. When he was finally ready to march, he had thirty-two thousand men.

But God came to Gideon again and said, "You have too many! With so large an army, they will take credit for winning the battle instead of saying, 'It was God who gave us the victory.' "

"What do you want me to do?" asked Gideon.

God answered, "Tell everybody who is afraid to go home."

When Gideon did this, twenty-two thousand did go home, leaving ten thousand who stayed.

"You still have too many," said God to Gideon. "Bring the men down to the spring, and I will test them again."

So Gideon led the ten thousand to the spring. Then God said to him, "All the men who lay their swords down, and get on their knees to drink, put on one side. Then everyone who keeps his sword in one hand and scoops the water up to his mouth in his other hand, put on the other side." Gideon watched, and only three hundred kept their swords in hand as they drank. "By the three hundred men who remained watchful and on guard, I will save you," said God to Gideon. "Send the rest back home."

That night Gideon divided his three hundred men into three companies—one hundred in each company. Each man carried a sword and each was given a trumpet, a lighted torch, and a large pitcher.

"Now," said Gideon, "each man is to do as I do. We will cover our torches with the pitchers and surround the camp of the Midianites on three sides. The side toward the river we will leave open. When I give the signal, we will all blow our trumpets, break our pitchers, wave our torches, and shout, 'The sword of the Lord and of Gideon!' "

Quietly they crept forward through the darkness. When Gideon knew his men had all arrived where they were told to go, he put his trumpet to his lips and blew a loud blast. His three hundred men blew their trumpets, too. Then all of them broke their pitchers, making a frightful noise. They waved their torches and shouted as loud as they could, "The sword of the Lord and of Gideon!"

Aroused from their sleep by these wild noises and seeing the flaming torches, the Midianites were really frightened! Thinking they were being attacked by a large army, they began to flee in the one direction Gideon had left open, down toward the Jordan river. All the while Gideon's three hundred men kept blowing their trumpets, shouting, and waving their torches. In the darkness and confusion, the Midianites could not tell friend from foe and found themselves fighting with one another as they fled pell-mell down the valley.

Gideon's Men March on the Midianites

Before long, several thousand of the men Gideon had sent home came back and joined in the fighting. Many Midianites, including their two kings, were killed. The rest were driven all the way back to their own country. So great was the victory of Gideon and his brave men that never again did the Midianites dare to come back into the land of Israel.

Later the people were so grateful to Gideon for what he had done that they came to him and said, "You shall be our king, and after you, your son, then your grandson, because you have saved us from the Midianites."

But Gideon said, "No, I will not be your king, nor shall my son rule over you. The Lord shall be your King, for it is He who has delivered you from your enemies, and He whom you should worship and serve forever."

Prayer

Dear God, my enemies are not people, but my temptations. Help me to be as brave in taking my stand against them as Gideon was in fighting the Midianites. Help me to know that You are the one who gives the victory, for I cannot do it with my own power. In Jesus' name, amen.

★ ★ ★ ★ ★ ★ ★ ★

QUESTIONS ON CHAPTER FIFTEEN

1. When Gideon called for men to join his army, how many came?

2. Why did God say that was too many?
3. How did Gideon reduce the number of men the first time? The second time?
4. How many men were left?
5. What did each of these soldiers carry into battle?
6. Describe their attack on the Midianites and the result.
7. If you were a soldier, and the commander said, "Whoever is afraid, go home," would you admit it if you were afraid?
8. Are there times when you are afraid, but you're also afraid to tell anyone? What can you do about it?
9. What are some of the temptations you need to fight against every day?
10. What does God provide to help us win? (See Ephesians 6:10-18.)

Chapter Sixteen

FIRST DAY IN SCHOOL

I am sure you know how happy your father and mother were the day you were born, and how they thanked God for you. But did you ever stop to think how much they wanted you and how many times they prayed for you, even before you were born?

Well, in the Bible there is a story about a father and mother—their names were Elkanah and Hannah—who did all this for their little son, Samuel, plus one thing more.

★ ★ ★ ★ ★ ★ ★ ★

Elkanah, Hannah, and three-year-old Samuel were very tired. They were on their way to the tabernacle in Shiloh and had been traveling all day. As they reached the top of the next hill, Elkanah said: "Look, there in the valley is a grove of trees. Nearby there must be a spring. That's where we will pitch our tent and spend the night."

Before long, they had finished their supper and were resting beside their campfire. "Samuel," said Hannah to her little son, "your father and I are so proud that you can grow up in God's house in Shiloh. We know you will be so much help to Eli, the priest, in his work in the tabernacle."

"But, Mother, what can I do?"

"Many things, my son. You can open the doors each morning, and sweep the floors. You can water the flowers and help take care of the garden. At night you can light the lamps. Later you can help the priest with the worship services. Eli will be your teacher. You will learn many things about God and His world and what God expects you to be."

"Mother, tell me again about the time you asked God for a son," said Samuel.

"Well, your father and I often asked God for a child. We had been married for several years, but we still had no children. Above everything else in all the world, we wanted a baby. So once, while we were at the tabernacle to offer our sacrifices, I went into the tabernacle to pray. I promised God that if He would send us a son, later I would bring him here so he could grow up under the care of the priest and be trained to do God's work. You are the gift God sent in answer to my prayer."

"That's why we named you Samuel," explained Elkanah. "Your name means 'asked of God.'"

"You will like Eli," said Hannah. "I will never forget how kind he was to me that day when I prayed in the tabernacle. As I was leaving, he put his hand on my head and said, 'Go in peace: and may God answer your prayer.' And now, Samuel, it's time for us to go to sleep.''

The next day, when they arrived in Shiloh, they took the bull they had brought along and sacrificed it to the Lord, as they did every year. Then they went to see Eli. "This is our little son, Samuel," said Elkanah after Eli had greeted them.

"What a fine boy," he said. "How I wish I could find someone like him to live with me and help me with my duties here."

"That is the reason we have come," said Hannah. "I promised God when I prayed for a son that, if He answered my prayer, I would bring him here to be His servant in the tabernacle."

Eli was very pleased. "I will take care of you as if you were my own son," Eli said to Samuel. "Perhaps you will grow up to be a prophet."

"What is a prophet?" Samuel asked.

"A man who speaks to the people for God," answered Eli, "a man who helps them to know God and to understand what God wants them to do."

"I think I would like to be a prophet when I grow up," said Samuel.

"Before Elkanah and I go back home," said Hannah, "may we go inside the tabernacle and show Samuel the place where I asked God to send us a son?"

Hannah Presents Samuel to Eli

"Of course," said Eli. He turned to lead the way. At the door he stopped. "Samuel," he said, "you are my helper now; so you may open the door." That pleased Samuel very much. When they came to the place where Hannah had prayed before, Eli asked them all to kneel. Then he prayed for God to bless all of them, especially Samuel in his new home and his new work. Do you understand why that spot ever after was to Samuel a very special place in the tabernacle, and why he so often knelt there to pray during the years that followed?

After Hannah and Elkanah had left for home, Eli stooped down and put his arm around Samuel and said, "You have such a wonderful father and mother! I'm sure you're going to be just the boy I need and that you will become the prophet God needs."

So Samuel lived with his friend and teacher, Eli the priest, in Shiloh and helped him every day with his duties in the tabernacle. As they worked together, week after week, Samuel learned not only about God, but about the needs of the people as they came to worship.

This was God's way of preparing him to become the great and good prophet he later did become—a prophet so loved and honored that two of the books in our Bible are named for him!

Prayer

Dear God, I thank you for parents who loved and prayed for me before I was born, and for the way I have been loved and cared for ever since. I thank you, too, for teachers who have helped me to know more about You and Your world so I can become the person You want me to be. Give me the joy of always doing my best. In Jesus' name, amen.

★ ★ ★ ★ ★ ★ ★ ★

QUESTIONS ON CHAPTER SIXTEEN

1. Why did Elkanah and Hannah bring Samuel to Eli?
2. What did Samuel learn from Eli?
3. What do you suppose were some things Samuel did to help Eli?
4. What are some of the things you can do for your church?
5. Ask your father or mother to tell you what they said to God when you were born and their hopes for you.
6. What can you do to help make their hopes come true?
7. Discuss some of the ways people give their full time to God's work today.

Chapter Seventeen

SURPRISE PACKAGE

Where do you go to school? Most likely you go to a school not far from where you live. So you are at home every night. But suppose for some reason your parents enrolled you in a boarding school several hundred miles away. Suppose, too, that they were very poor and were able to come to visit you only once a year. What could they do and what could you do to keep your love alive and warm?

Samuel grew up in the tabernacle. His mother, Hannah, had promised God if He would give her a son, she would give her son back to Him, and so it happened. Samuel's parents visited him every year when they offered sacrifices. They were proud of him as he served as Eli's helper, and he loved them very much.

★ ★ ★ ★ ★ ★ ★

It had been a busy day for Samuel. Hundreds of people had come to Shiloh to offer their sacrifices at the tabernacle. All day long Samuel had helped Eli, the priest, to greet them and to prepare the sacrifices.

Now that night had come, he was tired but happy—happy because among those who had come to Shiloh were his father and mother, Elkanah and Hannah. At last, he could sit down and talk with them.

"Son," said Elkanah, "we can see that you are a great help to Eli."

"He told us this morning that he couldn't get along without you," Hannah added. "We are proud of you, Samuel."

"Eli is very kind to me; I try to help him all I can."

Then Hannah gave Samuel a little package. "It's a present from us," she said.

"Oh, Mother!" Samuel exclaimed, as he opened it. It was a little, brown woolen coat! His mother had made it with her own hands—for in that day there were no factories or stores.

"Something to keep you warm," said Hannah, as she put it on him.

"And it fits me too!" exclaimed Samuel, all excited.

"It will remind you of how much we love you," Hannah said.

"I already knew that, and I love you, too," Samuel replied, as he threw his arms around them and kissed them.

"Listen, Samuel," Hannah said. "Mother is going to make you a promise. Since you are away from home, helping Eli and serving God in the tabernacle, I am going to bring you a

Samuel Gets a New Coat

new coat every year." And Hannah kept her promise! She brought Samuel a new coat every year when she and Elkanah came to Shiloh to worship in the tabernacle. Then the three of them would sit and have a nice long visit. Samuel would tell his parents what he and Eli had been doing, and his parents would tell him about back home. As they had more children, they would bring them along so Samuel could meet his brothers and sisters.

On one of these visits, they began to discuss Eli. "He seemed very sad when we saw him this morning," Elkanah said. "Do you think he is worried about something?"

"Yes, I know he is," answered Samuel. "He is worried about his two sons, Hophni and Phinehas. They steal from the people who come to the tabernacle and do many other things they should not do. A few nights ago, God told me about them."

"Tell us about it," said Hannah.

"I had just gone to bed," Samuel began, "when I heard someone calling my name. I thought it was Eli; so I jumped up and ran to him. But he said he had not called. Two more times I heard the voice and went to Eli. Each time he said he had not called me. The third time he said, 'Samuel, perhaps it is God's voice. If He calls again, say, "Speak, Lord, for I am your servant, and I am listening." '

"When I had gone back and was in bed again, I heard the voice calling. I said,

'Speak, Lord, for I am your servant, and I am listening.' Then God told me that Eli's two sons were very wicked and that He would never allow them to take their father's place as priests in the tabernacle."

"Does Eli know about this?" Elkanah asked.

"Yes," said Samuel. "The next morning he asked me about it; so I told him."

"No wonder he is sad," Elkanah said. "What a heavy burden—to have two sons like that."

"I am so glad that we do not have to worry about you, Samuel," Hannah said, as she put her arms around him and gave him a hug.

"Perhaps it will be God's plan for you to take Eli's place someday," said Elkanah. "If so, I know you will not fail Him."

Samuel did grow up to be a great prophet, and he took the place of Eli, the priest. He had learned many lessons as he was growing up with Eli. He learned not to be like Eli's sons. He learned to love his parents, who also loved him very much. Who can say how much their yearly visits and their love made Samuel the man he became? And who can say how much the loving care of our parents helps us to become the men and women God wants us to be?

Prayer

Dear God, thank you for parents, teachers,

and friends who show their love for me by being kind. Thank you for the many ways they help and encourage me. Help me to show how grateful I am by being kind to them and to all who need help that I can give. In Jesus' name, amen.

★ ★ ★ ★ ★ ★ ★ ★

QUESTIONS ON CHAPTER SEVEN-TEEN

1. Why was Eli worried?
2. What did God tell Samuel when He called to him? If you had been Samuel, how would you have felt about God's message to you?
3. What are some of the things you can do to make life happier for older people?
4. Why did "the little coat" mean so much to Samuel?
5. What were some of the ways he showed his gratitude for his parents' love?
6. List some of the gifts from your mother and your father to you.
7. In what ways can you show them that you are really grateful?
8. List some of God's gifts to you.
9. How can you show God how grateful you are?

THE RELUCTANT KING

The people of the United States have what is called a "presidential election" every four years. At that time, the people go to places called "the polls" and vote. In this way, they decide who will be the next president of the United States.

But for several months before the election, the men who want to be president (they are called "candidates") go around the country making speeches. From these speeches, it is clear that each "candidate" wants to be elected. But they often sound very proud and arrogant.

Well, what do you suppose would happen if one of them should say instead that he didn't feel worthy of the honor? Would that be a sign that he would make a good president?

Many years ago, the people of Israel were trying to decide whether to have a king or not to have a king. Almost everyone was for the idea, but Samuel was against it.

Samuel was their prophet, and usually they

looked to him for guidance. He warned them of how much it would cost to support a king and his court, but still they wanted one. He said God was their king, but they wanted a human king.

"We need someone to fight our battles and to defend us against our enemies," they said. "Besides, other nations have kings, and we want to be like them."

So Samuel gave in and promised that, with God's help, he would find them one. Then he asked God to help him to find and to choose the right man. "Tomorrow I will send him to you," God answered.

Sure enough, the next afternoon, Samuel saw a young man, whom he had never seen before, coming with his servant up the hill toward his house. Samuel noticed that he was very tall and handsome. Then a voice said, "This is the man I have chosen, the one who will be the king of my people."

The man's name was Saul, and for three days, he and his servant had walked here and there over the country searching for some donkeys that had strayed away from his father's farm. To every person they met, they said, "Have you seen any stray donkeys anywhere?" No one had. So on this, the afternoon of the third day, Saul said to his servant, "I don't like to give up, but by this time, my father will be worrying about us. Perhaps we had better go back home."

But the servant said, "I have heard that nearby, in the town of Ramah, lives a prophet who is a wise man of God. Perhaps he can help us find the donkeys."

"A good idea," Saul replied.

So they took the road to Ramah. When they arrived, the first person they met was Samuel, but, of course, they did not know who he was.

"Pardon me, sir," said Saul. "Can you tell us where the prophet lives?"

"I am the prophet," Samuel answered, "and over there is my house. Come with me up this hill. The whole city has been invited to a feast. You will be my guests. Do not worry about the donkeys that were lost. They are already back at your father's home. Tomorrow you can leave, and I will tell you whatever you want to know. But today, come to the feast, for all Israel wants to know you."

Saul could not believe it! How did Samuel know about the donkeys before they asked him? And why would all Israel want to meet *him*? "But I am from the tribe of Benjamin," he said, "the smallest of all the twelve tribes of Israel. My family is one of the least known in our tribe! Why do you say something like that to me?"

But Samuel didn't answer. He just led the way to the feast. So Saul went to dinner with Samuel. There, to his great surprise, he was given the chief seat and was served first—as if the dinner had been prepared in his honor! And he spent the night in the house of Samuel.

The next morning when Saul and his servant were ready to leave, Samuel walked with them a little way. When they came to the edge of the city, he asked Saul to send his servant on ahead. Then, from his coat he took a small flask of oil and poured it on Saul's head, saying as he did, "God has anointed you to be the king and captain of His people! He will be with you to help you."

Several days later, Samuel called the people together in the city of Mizpah, where he promised to introduce them to their new king.

When the day arrived, a great crowd was there, listening. Samuel said, "I promised to find a man to be your king. Then I asked God to lead me to the right man, and He has answered my prayer. The one whom He has chosen is from the tribe of Benjamin. His father's name is Kish, and his name is Saul. I ask him to come now and stand beside me that all of you may see and welcome him."

Of course, eyes were turned in all directions; everyone wanted to see the new king! But, would you believe it? Saul did not come forward! Once again, the feeling of humility and unworthiness had come over him, and he had slipped away to hide. No one could find him!

Samuel Anoints Saul

Then God spoke to Samuel: "Have someone look in the tent where the baggage is."

Sure enough, there he was! And when he came out, everyone saw that he was six or eight inches taller than anyone else. From all sides, words of praise and admiration were heard:

"How tall he is!" said one.

"And strong!" a second said.

"And handsome!" a third exclaimed.

"Just the right man!" a fourth shouted.

When at last he was standing by Samuel, Samuel laid his hand upon Saul's shoulder and said: "This is the man God has chosen to be your king. See for yourselves that not one of you can be compared to him!"

The people agreed as they raised their hands high in the air and shouted at the top of their voices: "God save the king! God save the king!"

Thus Saul, the son of Kish, became the first king of the nation of Israel. What a great honor! But, also, what a great responsibility!

Prayer

Dear God, if I am ever chosen for something special, may it make me feel humble and grateful, but not proud. Then may I do my best not to fail, and may I trust you to help me. And thank you for all the times you have already helped me. In Jesus' name, amen.

QUESTIONS ON CHAPTER EIGHTEEN

1. Why did the people of Israel ask for a king? When is it hardest for you to do things God's way and not be "like everyone else"?

2. What did Samuel say before he gave in to them?

3. How did God bring it about that Saul and Samuel should meet when and where they did?

4. Why did Saul hesitate to accept the honor of becoming king?

5. Make a list of the good qualities you find in Saul as you think back upon this story.

6. Why are proud people not more popular?

7. Why should you be humble and not proud about the gifts God has given you?

8. What can you do to keep from being too proud?

Chapter Nineteen

WHEN THE LAST WAS FIRST

If you were left out of something you very much wanted to be a part of because you were too young or too little, how would you feel? Well, if you were a good sport about it and didn't grumble or complain, then later found it all turned out for the best, that would make it okay, wouldn't it?

That's just what happened to a shepherd boy named David.

★ ★ ★ ★ ★ ★ ★ ★

David loved all seven of his brothers, but sometimes he wished he were not the youngest. Often, when his brothers were starting to play a game or planning to go somewhere, one would say, "You are too little, David," and he would be left out. Even when he was older, whenever "someone" had to stay, he was always the one.

On one particular morning, more than anything in all the world, he wanted to be in Bethlehem. Everybody in and around the town was excited because the prophet

Samuel was coming to offer a special sacrifice to God, and it was rumored that at noon he would announce who would be the next king of Israel. But that morning, his father, Jesse, said, "David, someone must take care of the sheep. I want you to do that today while we go to the sacrifice."

David did as he was told. He did not argue with his father. But all that morning, as the sheep were grazing in the valley, he was sitting under a tree playing his harp, wondering what was going on in Bethlehem and wishing he could be there.

He had just finished his lunch when he saw two of his brothers, Abinadab and Shammah, running over the hill toward him. Abinadab was shouting, "David, David, come quick!"

"I will stay and watch the sheep," said Shammah. "You go with Abinadab."

As they hurried along, Abinadab told David what had happened back in Bethlehem.

"Soon after the prophet Samuel arrived," he said, "he came over to our father and said: 'Jesse, God has revealed to me that one of your sons is to be the next king of Israel. I want you to bring them to me, one by one.'

"Eliab came first. We all thought he would be the one, because he is the oldest, the tallest, and very handsome. But the prophet said: 'God has not chosen him.' Then he added: 'People look on the outside of a man, but God looks on the heart.'

"I was next, then Shammah, then our four other brothers, but in each case, Samuel said, 'This is not the one.'

"At last he turned to our father and said: 'Are these all your sons?' Then Father told him about you, and the prophet said: 'Send for him. We will not offer the sacrifice until he comes.' "

At last Abinadab and David arrived, red-faced and panting, and made their way through the crowd to where Samuel and Jesse were standing beside the altar.

"This is my youngest son. His name is David," Jesse said to Samuel.

"David," said Samuel, "before I came to Bethlehem, God revealed to me that one of your father's sons would be the next king of Israel, but I did not know which one. All seven of your brothers have come before me. In each case, God said, 'This is not the one.' But when you came, God said, 'Rise and anoint him, for he is the one.' God has chosen you; one day you will be king of Israel."

Then David dropped to his knees, and Samuel poured oil upon his head, saying, "May the Lord bless you and make you a good king." After that, it didn't trouble David anymore that he was the youngest in his family. Later he did become, as Samuel had prayed, a noble king, one known far and wide as "a man after God's own heart."

Samuel Anoints David

Prayer

Dear God, no matter how young or little I am, I believe You have a noble plan for my life. Help me to be a good student at school and a happy helper at home so I will be prepared to fulfill your will with my life. In Jesus' name, amen.

★ ★ ★ ★ ★ ★ ★ ★

QUESTIONS ON CHAPTER NINE-TEEN

1. Why did Samuel come to Bethlehem?
2. Why was one of Jesse's older sons not chosen?
3. What have you learned from this story about judging people by appearance?
4. Why was David not in town when Samuel came to Bethlehem? How did he feel about that?
5. Can you think of a time when you were disappointed about something, but later it turned out for the best? What happened?
6. What should that teach you about faith? About patience?
7. The Bible says that David was a "man after God's own heart" (see Acts 13:22). Do you think that could be said about you? Why or why not?
8. How do you believe God wants to use you in His work? What should you be doing now to be prepared?
9. How can you make every task "special"?

Chapter Twenty

SUPERBOY

Do you like stories about Batman, Tarzan, the Bionic Woman, and Superman? Well, did you ever stop to think that you don't have to be "bionic" to be "super"? The Bible tells us about a shepherd boy who proved he was really "super."

★ ★ ★ ★ ★ ★ ★ ★

One evening in Bethlehem, a man named Jesse called his son to his side. "David," he said, "tomorrow I want you to take a basket of food to your three brothers and find out how they are and how the battle is going."

Now King Saul was leading the army in a war with the Philistines, a war-like people who lived along the seashore of Palestine. These people often attacked the farms and villages of the people of Israel who lived in the hills. Saul intended to stop such raids; so David's three oldest brothers had joined Saul's army. It was to those brothers that David was being sent by his father.

David started early the next morning, went to the place where Saul's army was, and soon found his brothers. They were glad to have the food David had brought and also to hear the news from home.

Suddenly, a great shout was heard from the camp of the Philistines, which was across the valley on the opposite hill. David and his brothers could see the leader of the Philistines, a big giant named Goliath. He was walking back and forth in front of the Philistine camp, waving his sword high in the air, and shouting across the valley: "Choose your strongest man, and let him come over and fight with me. If he is able to kill me, then my people will become your slaves. But if I kill him, then your people will become our slaves. I dare any man to come over and fight me."

But the men in Saul's army were all afraid. Not one accepted the dare. To David, this was a disgrace. So he said to some of the soldiers, "I will go fight him."

When Eliab, his oldest brother, heard about it, he said: "Come on! You don't know anything about fighting! Go watch the sheep! Who do you think you are anyway?"

But when Saul heard about David's courage, he sent for him. When he saw David was younger than all his soldiers, he said: "You are too young and have never been in a battle. The giant has been a man of war for years."

"I'm not afraid of him," David replied, "and God will help me."

When Saul saw David was determined, he gave him his armor—a sword, a bronze helmet, and a coat of mail. When David tried them on, they swallowed him! So he put them aside and started down the hill with his shepherd's staff in one hand and his sling in the other.

Do you wonder why he decided to fight the giant? I think it was because he knew that God had chosen him to be the next king of Israel. Samuel, the prophet, had already anointed him in Bethlehem. He felt he must be brave and strong and not allow Goliath to get away with his dare.

That sling he carried at his side was one he had made with his own hands. He had practiced and practiced with it until he could hit the target almost every time. At the foot of the hill was a stream, and in the bed of the stream were many small stones.

His father had taught him what kind of stones were best for slings; so he was very careful about the ones he selected. He found five that were smooth and round, about the size of an egg. These he placed in a little bag tied to his waist. Then he started up the hill toward the giant. Saul and his army were watching in spellbound silence from the hill behind him.

Now Goliath's entire body was covered with armor, and he held a spear in one hand and a sword in the other. When he saw

David, he laughed out loud and made fun of him: "Boy, how did you ever get away from your mother? Am I a dog that you come to me with a stick and a hand full of rocks? Why, I will feed you to the birds and wild animals!"

David answered back, "You come against me with a sword and a spear, but I come against you in the name of the Lord God of Israel, whom you have defied. He is on our side, and He will give me the victory over you so that all these people may know that He is the true God. I am not afraid of you, because God is with us!"

David slipped one of the stones into his sling and began whirling it around and around. He noticed, as Goliath came closer, that there was a spot right between his eyes not covered by his armor. So straight for that spot he aimed as Goliath rushed at him.

Swift and true the stone sped to its mark, hitting the giant right between the eyes. That stopped him cold! He stood still for a second, then fell forward on his face.

At that moment, there went up a mighty shout from behind David as the army of Israel rushed forward toward the Philistine camp. The Philistines, seeing that their leader had fallen, started running pell-mell in the opposite direction with Israel hot in pursuit.

So because of the courage and skill of David, the army of Israel won a great victory

David Kills Goliath with a Sling

that day over the Philistines. For many weeks afterward on all sides, people kept talking about David and singing his praises. But in all Israel no one was more pleased than the prophet Samuel, for he knew the day that David would become a brave and noble king could not be far away.

★ ★ ★ ★ ★ ★ ★ ★

Prayer

Dear God, help me to be as brave in meeting my temptations as David was in meeting Goliath. May I remember that I never have to fight alone, but that You are always ready to help me just as You helped David. Teach me too, that no temptation is too strong if I use my willpower and Your help. In Jesus' name, amen.

★ ★ ★ ★ ★ ★ ★ ★

QUESTIONS ON CHAPTER TWENTY

1. Why did David go to the camp of Saul's army?
2. What made Saul's soldiers so afraid?
3. Why did King Saul send for David?
4. What qualities do you see in David that make him worthy to be called "super"?
5. What was the secret of his courage? How can you have that kind of courage?
6. What was the secret of his skill with a sling?
7. What are some of the enemies you must conquer if you are to become a superboy or a supergirl?

Chapter Twenty-one

THE BEST OF FRIENDS

When we say of someone, "He is a good sport," what do we mean? Perhaps two things: (1) When he succeeds, he does not become proud and boastful. (2) When he fails, he does not become angry or complain. The Bible tells us about two young men who not only were the best of friends; they were good sports toward each other as long as they lived.

★ ★ ★ ★ ★ ★ ★ ★

When David came back to the camp after his victory over the giant Goliath, King Saul, who had watched the battle, asked that he be brought to his tent so he could reward him for his brave deed.

Then Saul introduced him to another young man standing beside him: "This is my son, Jonathan. You and he should become good friends because to reward you for what you have done, I am going to take you home with us. Your brothers who are in my army may return to Bethlehem and tell your father."

"Whatever the king says, I will do," David replied.

Then Jonathan shook hands with David and said, "David, I am glad to be your friend!" And Jonathan really meant it, for the Bible tells us, "From that time, his soul was knit to the soul of David, and he loved him as his own soul"—which means that he really loved him as much as he loved himself!

In a way, it was strange that Jonathan and David should become such close friends, because, you see, they were *rivals*. Both were in line to become the next king of Israel. Jonathan was in line because he was the son of Saul, Israel's first king. David was in line because in Bethlehem, the prophet Samuel had anointed him before a great crowd and had declared that he was God's choice to be the next king. Of course, Saul had not heard about this when he took David home with him.

For a while, Saul was good to David. He made him an officer in his army, and God made everything David did go well. But as the people kept on praising David, Saul began to be jealous of his popularity. One evening, as David was playing his harp in the palace (he was a fine musician as well as a brave soldier), Saul, in a fit of anger, threw his spear at him, trying to kill him. But David escaped.

Then Saul sent David to battle, captain over more than a thousand men. He did this because he hoped David would be killed in battle. When that didn't work, he promised that David could marry his daughter if he first killed 100 Philistines. But the truth was, he hoped David would be killed by the Philistines.

But David was successful in fighting the Philistines, killed 200 of them, and married Saul's daughter. Then Saul told his servants and Jonathan to kill David. But Jonathan warned David. Then he went to Saul and spoke well of David to him. And Saul listened to his son Jonathan, and David was allowed to return to be with Saul as before.

Again war broke out, and David went with the army. He was so successful that Saul again became jealous. A second time he threw his spear at David while he was playing his harp. Again David escaped, and he knew he had to stay away for good this time.

Before he left, he found Jonathan and said: "Jonathan, why does your father try to kill me? What have I done wrong?"

"You have done nothing wrong," Jonathan assured him. "I don't think my father really wants to kill you. He tells me everything, and he has said nothing of killing you."

But David replied, "Your father knows we are friends. He doesn't want to hurt you by letting you know, but I'm sure he wants to kill me."

"Whatever you want me to do, I'll do it," said Jonathan.

"Jonathan," David said. "You are a true and wonderful friend. I thank God for you! Tomorrow I am supposed to eat with your father. When he asks why I'm not there, speak kindly about me. If he doesn't get angry, then we'll know I am safe. But if he loses his temper, I must escape."

"I will talk to him," Jonathan said. "I know God has chosen you to be the next king, and I am sure you will be a good king."

Then they made a covenant together and promised each other that no matter what happened, they would always be true friends. After that, David left and hid in a large field.

Two days later, when he still hadn't shown up at the palace for meals, Saul asked where he was. This was Jonathan's chance to say a good word for him. "Father," he said, "you shouldn't be angry with David; he is loyal to you and has never done anything against you. Don't you remember how you felt about him and praised him when he was so brave and went out to fight Goliath?"

But Saul became very angry. He called Jonathan an ugly name, and shouted, "That's enough, Jonathan! Can't you see it will cost you your crown if you keep on being David's friend? As long as he is alive, you will never be king. That is why he must die!"

"Father," said Jonathan, "I would rather keep David for my friend than to become king."

David and Jonathan Say Goodbye

At that, Saul's anger exploded, and he threw his spear at Jonathan! Jonathan left the table without eating and went out to the field. There he found David and told him what had happened. Both of them were very troubled and again promised each other that they would always be true friends.

"Jonathan," David said, "I cannot tell you what you mean to me. But this I promise:if God keeps me alive and I do become king, you will be next to me in my kingdom!"

David really meant that promise. He did later become king, but before that time, sad to say, Jonathan had been killed fighting bravely in a battle against the Philistines. But long after Jonathan was dead, David still remembered him and loved him.

Prayer

Dear God, help me to remember that the way to have friends is to be friendly. Then make me as kind and unselfish toward my friends as Jonathan was to David. And thank You, dear God, for the kind of friend You are to me. In Jesus' name, amen.

★ ★ ★ ★ ★ ★ ★ ★

QUESTIONS ON CHAPTER TWENTY-ONE

1. Why did Saul take David home with him?
2. Why did he later hate David?
3. What did David do when Saul tried to kill him?

4. What promise did David and Jonathan make to each other?

5. Could you be a friend to someone who got a job you wanted? How can you be more like Jonathan, who loved David even though David would become king instead of him?

6. Do you get angry or jealous easily? What can you do about it?

7. Why would you say Jonathan was "a good sport" toward David?

8. Why would you say David was "a good sport" toward Jonathan?

9. Which is harder, to be a good sport when you are a winner or when you are a loser? What makes it hard in both cases?

10. Thinking of David and Jonathan, how would you describe a true friend?

Chapter Twenty-two

A TRUE FRIEND NEVER FORGETS

"It pays to be kind." Do you agree with that? Perhaps we can't always say that, because sometimes it *costs* to be kind. It may cost time, or money, or sacrifice—like giving a friend something you want for yourself. Or like standing up for someone who is being picked on, or being helpful to someone who is different.

But whether it pays or costs, one thing we know: it is always right to be kind. That is why we admire a person who is kind.

★ ★ ★ ★ ★ ★ ★ ★

Mephibosheth, the grandson of Saul, was really afraid! Why should David send for him? He had never seen David, but he knew he was a rich and powerful king. He knew, too, that his grandfather, Saul, had tried to kill David.

No wonder, then, after the death of his father and grandfather (both of them had been killed in the same battle, fighting against the Philistines), Mephibosheth had lived

130

quietly in hiding, hoping David would never find out where he was. But now the king's servants were at his door with a command to bring him to Jerusalem. He was afraid to go, but he dared not refuse.

"Why has the king sent for me?" he asked, as one of the servants helped him to mount the extra donkey they had brought.

"We don't know," replied the servant. "We were only told to bring you." So they rode away in silence.

When they arrived in Jerusalem, Mephibosheth was taken at once to the palace into the presence of the king. David noticed that he was trembling. "Mephibosheth," he said, "why are you so afraid? No one is going to harm you."

"But, my grandfather, when he was king, was cruel to you," answered Mephibosheth. "He wanted my father, Jonathan, to be king after him. Several times he tried to kill you, and I thought perhaps you remembered and—"

"Say no more," David broke in. "I have forgotten that long ago. Your grandfather was a sick man. Besides, didn't you know your father was my best friend?"

"My father died when I was only five years old," said Mephibosheth. "He was killed fighting the Philistines."

"Yes," replied David. "He was very brave! Also the most unselfish man ever."

King David Is Kind to Mephibosheth

"Why do you say he was unselfish?" said Mephibosheth.

"Because of how kind he was to me," David answered. "You see, Mephibosheth, since Jonathan was the oldest son of Saul, he naturally expected to be king after his father. But when he heard that God's prophet, Samuel, had anointed me to be the next king, he was not the least bit angry or jealous. Instead, he did everything he could to help me. More than once he saved my life! If your father had lived, I would have given him the highest office in my kingdom. I loved him as if he were my own brother. That is why I have sent for you, Mephibosheth. I want to show you kindness for the sake of your father Jonathan!"

"For you to say these things about my father is kindness enough," said Mephibosheth.

"No, no," David continued. "I will do more! From this day on, my palace will be your home. You will eat at my table as if you were my own son. I will care for you as Jonathan would have done, had he lived!"

"But you forget," said Mephibosheth, "you forget I am lame. There are those who would say a cripple should not be in the palace."

"How long have you been lame?" asked David.

"Since the day my father died," Mephibosheth replied. "When a messenger arrived with the news that the Philistines had won the battle and that my father, as well as his father, had been killed, my nurse picked me up and ran from the house to carry me to a safe place. She stumbled and fell. Both of my ankles were broken. I was five years old and have been lame ever since. So you see, it is best that I go back home. Here I would be a burden to my lord, the king."

"You will not be a burden," said David. "I am giving back to you all the land that belonged to King Saul; it would have been your father's if he had lived."

Then David called for one of his best servants. "Mephibosheth, this is Ziba. He was once a servant of your grandfather, Saul. From now on, he will be your servant, and he has twenty other servants to help him. Over these you will be master. They will care for the land which I am now giving you. The fruit and the harvest shall be yours."

Then David added, "Mephibosheth, in you I see your father's friendly eyes and his warm, unselfish spirit. It will mean much to me to have you near. No one could be more welcome in my court than Jonathan's son."

So Mephibosheth was given the land that had been Saul's, lived in the palace at Jerusalem as if he were the king's son, and had his meals at the king's table, as long as he lived! In this way, David repaid the kindness

Jonathan had shown him many years earlier. He proved that a true friend never forgets.

★ ★ ★ ★ ★ ★ ★ ★

Prayer

Dear God, teach me to be truly thankful for all the kindness I have received from others, and make me kind to everyone I know. There is much selfishness and cruelty in the world and many troubled people. May I show that I care by doing everything I can to help others. In Jesus' name, amen.

★ ★ ★ ★ ★ ★ ★ ★

QUESTIONS ON CHAPTER TWENTY-TWO

1. Why was Mephibosheth afraid when David sent for him?
2. How did Mephibosheth become crippled?
3. Why did David invite him to live in the palace?
4. Name a kind thing someone once did for you. How did you show your gratitude?
5. Name a kind thing you once did for someone else. Why did you do it?
6. Can you think of someone to whom you should be kind for the same reason David was kind to Mephibosheth?
7. Are you thoughtful about being kind to others who are different from you?
8. Can you think of a kind deed you can do every day this week?

Chapter Twenty-three

NO VACANCY

If you were traveling across the country with your family, where would you expect to spend the night? Perhaps in a motel?

But suppose you had car trouble, and it was after dark when you arrived in the town where you planned to stop, and the motels were all full—"No Vacancy" signs everywhere! What would you do?

Would you be willing to sleep in a barn if someone offered it to you? Perhaps so, if you were very, very tired and there were nowhere else to go.

Many years ago something like that happened to a Jewish family in a faraway country, and the day it happened has been remembered ever since!

★ ★ ★ ★ ★ ★ ★ ★

Simeon, owner of the inn in Bethlehem, had mixed feelings about the new national census ordered by the Roman emperor. He knew it meant higher taxes for him and for his fellow Jews throughout the land of Palestine. That he did not like! But it also meant more business for his inn, and that he did like!

136

For days ahead, he and his servants were busy gathering in supplies. By noon on the day before the registration was to begin, most of his rooms were already taken, and people were still crowding into the city. Early in the afternoon, Simeon put up the "No Vacancy" sign—his inn was full.

Simeon was very happy about that. Most of his guests were wealthy and spent their money freely, ordering food and wine. The jingle of silver and gold coins dropping into his purse was music to Simeon's ears. Already he was one of the richest men in Bethlehem. But still something was missing!

Shortly after dark, a man and woman opened the door and came over to where he sat counting his money. At a glance, he saw that they were poor and very tired. Also, the woman looked as if she were in pain.

It was the man who spoke: "My name is Joseph, and this is my wife, Mary. We have come from Nazareth in Galilee to register in the census. We need lodging for the night."

"Sorry," Simeon replied, "my rooms are all taken. Surely you saw the 'No Vacancy' sign on the door!"

"It is urgent," Joseph pleaded. "Please don't turn us away. My wife is exhausted, and tonight her baby may be born!"

A woman about to have a baby! That was the last thing Simeon wanted at a time like this. The struggle in his conscience was short.

"My good man, I am very sorry. But as I have already said, my inn is full!" And he stood up to indicate the interview was over.

But it was not over! Just then, the woman, pale and weary, fainted into her husband's arms. Gently he laid her on the floor, pulling off his cloak to make a pillow for her head.

As Simeon looked down at her pale but beautiful face, his heart was troubled. "My friend," he said to Joseph, "behind the inn is a cave used as a stable. The first stall is empty, with fresh, clean straw. You may spend the night there, if you wish." Mary was reviving. With a tear, she whispered, "Oh, thank you." Simeon had to turn his eyes away. He ordered a servant to show them to the stable and to get them a candle, a pitcher of water, and some food. Then he turned to take care of his guests, who were calling loudly for more wine.

It was almost midnight when he went up to bed. The back window of his room opened out toward the stable. He noticed that a light was still burning in the first stall. He wondered about the woman and whether or not the baby had arrived.

But why should he be concerned? He had his other guests to think about—his *paying* guests! He could not be responsible for every expectant mother and every newborn baby in the world! Shrugging his shoulders, he threw himself on his bed. Soon he was fast asleep!

Two or three hours later, he was awakened by the sound of voices coming from the direction of the stable. Fearing that the guests in his inn might be disturbed, he threw a cloak over his shoulders and rushed out.

To his amazement, he found a number of shepherds crowding into the stable to see the newborn baby. Joseph and Mary were listening in rapt silence as the shepherds told why they had come.

"We were out under the stars guarding our sheep. Suddenly a company of angels appeared in the sky. They were singing: 'Glory to God in the highest.' One of the angels said: 'This day, in the city of David, a Savior is born who is Christ, the Lord. And this will be a sign for you: you will find the baby wrapped in cloths and lying in a manger.' So we came as fast as we could."

As Simeon listened to that amazing story and looked down into the face of the newborn baby, his heart melted. He had come to drive the shepherds away. Now he felt as they did!

But why hadn't the angel come to him? Had he known that the baby was to be the Savior of the world, he would have found room for Joseph and Mary in the inn. He would have given them his own room.

Was it because he had been too busy thinking about money and trying to make more and more? Was it because he hadn't found time to look at the stars or to think about angels or

Simeon Visits the Stable

God, or about how much the world needed a Savior?

After the shepherds left, Simeon spoke kindly to Joseph and Mary. He asked for their forgiveness and invited them to come back to the inn and take his room. "I can sleep on a couch in the hall," he said. "I should have thought of that before."

Joseph assured him he was forgiven but declined his invitation. "My wife is not yet strong enough to walk," he said. "We are all right here. As you said, the stable is clean, and the hay in the manger is fresh. The baby is already asleep."

"He is truly a beautiful child," said Simeon. "Have you decided on His name?"

"God made that decision for us," replied Joseph. "Several months ago, an angel appeared to me, also to Mary at a different time, and said: 'You shall call Him Jesus (which means "Savior") because He will save His people from their sins.' "

Those words of Joseph spoke straight to the greatest need in the life of Simeon. So he stepped over to the manger where the baby Jesus was sleeping and, bowing his head, asked God to forgive him for his selfishness and unkindness in sending Joseph and Mary out to the stable and for all his other sins. Then he said, "Good night and God bless you," to the three of them and left.

Somehow, as he went up to his room and to

bed, his conscience wasn't troubling him anymore. His heart was filled with great joy.

★ ★ ★ ★ ★ ★ ★ ★ ★

Prayer

Dear God,
"Don't let my heart be a busy inn,
That has no room for Thee;
But a cradle for the baby Jesus
And His nativity." (Cushman, adapted)
In Jesus' name, amen.

★ ★ ★ ★ ★ ★ ★ ★ ★

QUESTIONS ON CHAPTER TWENTY-THREE

1. How did Simeon feel about the new census? Why?
2. What was it like at the inn on the day before the census?
3. Who were the travellers who arrived late and asked for a room?
4. Who was the baby born that night? How did He get His name? What does His name mean?
5. If you have guests at home and they spend the night, how do you feel about giving up your bed for them? Why do you suppose Simeon did not offer his bed to Mary and Joseph until later?
6. Why do you think the angels told the shepherds and not Simeon about Jesus?
7. What do you think Simeon did differently at his inn after he met Jesus?
8. How can you be less selfish?

Chapter Twenty-four

A STAR IS BORN

Have you ever looked up into the sky, picked out one of the stars as if it belonged to you, and said:

"Twinkle, twinkle little star,
How I wonder what you are,
Up above the world so high,
Like a diamond in the sky."

In the Bible is a story about a very special star. Whether it twinkled or not, we do not know. But the Bible tells us it moved, and some men who were said to be very wise followed it for days and days, or rather nights and nights, until it led them to—but let us not run ahead of the story.

★ ★ ★ ★ ★ ★ ★

Several miles outside the city of Jerusalem, three friends stood, each beside his camel, gazing into the night sky. Their names were Caspar, Balthazar, and Melchior, and they were troubled because, while the heavens were bright with stars, they could not find the one for which they were looking.

"Strange that it should lead us this far and then disappear," said Caspar.

143

"Perhaps this is God's way of telling us that we are almost there," Balthazar added. "Maybe Jerusalem is the place. That is where one would expect a new king of the Jews to be born."

They were silent for a moment, then Melchior said: "Tomorrow we can go into the city and inquire whether anyone knows about the birth of a new prince."

Caspar, Balthazar, and Melchior were not only friends but were diligent students of the stars. For this reason, they were known as "Magi," or "Wise-men." Back in Persia, the land from which they had come, they had often discussed with Hebrew scholars certain passages in the Hebrew Scriptures where prophets had spoken of a king who would some day come and bring justice and peace to the world. There was one prophecy in particular that connected His coming with the appearance of a new star. It read:

"I see him, but not now; I behold him, but not near. A star will come out of Jacob; a scepter will rise out of Israel" (Numbers 24:17, *New International Version,* copyright 1978, New York International Bible Society, used by permission; hence noted NIV).

The three Wise-men had come to believe that the new star they had discovered in the sky was the very one the Hebrew prophecy was speaking about. So they had left their native land of Persia and, for several weeks, had followed the star as it moved across the sky.

They had sold a great part of their possessions in order to buy a train of camels and provisions for the journey. Also, each had purchased a rich present to give to the newborn king, if and when they should find Him.

They had come several hundred miles. They were very weary, but the appearance of the star every night had kept their hopes alive—that is, until now, when it was not to be seen anywhere.

Before they entered Jerusalem the next morning, King Herod's spies had already reported their presence outside the city. The Wise-men made a very impressive sight as they rode in on their colorfully decorated camels. They created a great deal of curiosity as they went here and there asking people, "Where is He who has been born King of the Jews? For we have seen His star in the East and have come to worship Him."

When Herod heard that, he knew it was time to act! He could not stand the thought of anyone's being king but himself!

So, covering up his fear and jealousy, he pretended to be friendly toward the Magi and invited them to his palace.

His invitation brought them a new spark of hope—"Maybe the newborn prince is Herod's son," they said to one another.

But no! His sons were grown men and as

unworthy to be king as Herod was! Of course the Magi, as yet, did not know this.

So when they were ushered into the presence of the king, they told him about the star and asked him whether he knew where the new king the Hebrew prophets had spoken about was to be born. "We have come from far away," they said, "to worship Him."

Herod, of course, did not know the answer to their question. But still pretending to be friendly, he summoned the Jewish religious scholars in the city and passed the question on to them. They quickly came up with the answer.

"In Bethlehem of Judea," they said, "for this is what the prophet Micah wrote: 'O little town of Bethlehem, you are not just an insignificant Jewish village. For from you shall come a ruler who will govern my people Israel.' "

Then Herod was really troubled! Sending away the religious scholars, he said to himself: "I am king, and king I intend to remain! No newborn baby in Bethlehem or anywhere else will get my throne!"

But to the three Magi, he said in a smooth voice, "When did this new star you have been following first appear?"

"Many nights ago when we were still in Persia," they said.

"And where is it now?" he asked.

"We do not know," they replied.

The Wise-men Talk with Herod

"Then go on to Bethlehem," he said cunningly. "Keep searching for the young child until you find Him, for according to our scholars, that is where He is to be born. And when you have found Him, come back and report to me, and I will go and worship Him, too."

The Magi did not know that in his evil heart, Herod was already planning to kill the baby! It was not worship he had in mind, but murder!

After they left the palace, they took the road to Bethlehem. Suddenly, there was the star again, going on before them! Their joy knew no bounds as they followed it on and on until it stopped above the very house where the baby Jesus was.

When they entered, what they saw was a carpenter, whose name was Joseph, and his wife Mary, and a sweet little child in her arms. But they knew this was the One they were seeking because the star that had led them all the way from Persia kept shining right above the house where they were! So they fell on their knees in worship and thanked God for having guided them all the way.

Then, going out to their camels, they unloaded the rich gifts they had brought and placed them in front of the baby. Caspar's gift was gold. Balthazar's was frankincense, while Melchior's was sweet-smelling myrrh.

Perhaps you are thinking, "What strange

gifts to bring to a little baby!'' And you are right. But, you see, Jesus was a very special baby! And through those gifts, God was revealing who Jesus was and why He had been sent into the world. The gold was a sign that He would some day be a king and that we should obey Him. The frankincense was a sign that He was divine, God's own Son, and that we should worship Him. The myrrh was a sign that He would later die on a cross to save us from our sins.

Thus, the presents the Wise-men brought were not strange gifts after all, but most appropriate, in view of who Jesus was and why God sent Him into the world. So we, as were Mary and Joseph, should be forever grateful for the gifts they chose and brought to the baby Jesus many long years ago.

★ ★ ★ ★ ★ ★ ★ ★

Prayer

"What can I give Him, poor as I am?

If I were a shepherd, I would give him a lamb,

If I were a Wise-man, I would do my part—

But what can I give Him? I will give Him my heart.'' (Christina Rossetti, adapted)

Dear God, help me to give my heart to Jesus. In Jesus' name, amen.

★ ★ ★ ★ ★ ★ ★ ★

QUESTIONS ON CHAPTER TWENTY-FOUR

1. Where were the three Wise-men at the

beginning of the story, and where had they come from?

2. Why were they troubled?
3. Why were they following a star?
4. What did they keep asking people the next morning in Jerusalem?
5. What would you think about three strangers in your town asking about a newborn king?
6. Why did Herod say he invited the Wise-men to his palace? What was his real reason?
7. What do you think about Herod's jealousy? What makes you jealous? How can you change that?
8. What gifts did the Wise-men bring Jesus? What did they mean?
9. If you were Joseph or Mary, what would you have thought about the three Wise-men stopping at your house? What would you have done with the gifts they brought?
10. What do you suppose the Wise-men thought when they discovered that the "King" they were looking for was in the home of a poor carpenter? How do you feel about poorer people?
11. What is the best gift you can bring to Jesus?

Chapter Twenty-five

MIXED BLESSINGS

What do we mean when we say of some experience that it is a "mixed blessing"? We mean that it has both a bright and a dark side.

For example, you were a "mixed blessing" to your parents when you were born.

On the bright side, they had new reasons for joy—your rosy little face, your sweet smile, the congratulations and good wishes of friends, and their hopes and dreams about your future.

But they had new concerns too—concerns about your food, your sleep, your health, your safety, and, later, concerns about your education, your friends, your habits, and your faith.

This same thing was true about the birth of Jesus. At the beginning, it was joy upon joy for Mary and Joseph.

But concerns were not long in coming.

When the Wise-men visited Herod the king, he asked them to come back to Jerusalem after they had found the newborn baby and tell him where the child was. He said he wanted to come and worship the child, too. But he really wanted to kill the baby! So God warned the Magi about Herod's plot, and they went back to their own country by another route.

Herod was furious when he found this out. He ordered his soldiers to go to Bethlehem and to kill every boy baby not yet two years old!

What a cruel thing for Herod to do! But that was his way of making sure that no new-born baby would ever become king instead of himself. So he thought! In the meantime, an angel had appeared to Joseph in a dream.

"Get up quickly," the angel said. "Take the child and His mother, and flee to the land of Egypt, for Herod is planning to kill Him."

So Joseph woke Mary up and told her about the dream. They hurried to get ready to leave. When they were ready, they picked up the baby Jesus and slipped away in the dark of the night.

The next day, Herod's soldiers did come to Bethlehem. They killed all the tiny boy babies. That was a very sad day for all the people in the town.

But Jesus was already on His way to the land of Egypt. There He and Mary and Joseph lived until the wicked Herod died. Then an angel appeared to Joseph in another dream and told him it was now safe for them to return to their own country.

So they set out from Egypt to go home again. To them, home was a village called Nazareth, in the province of Galilee some sixty miles north of Jerusalem.

On the way, coming up from the land of Egypt, Mary said to Joseph, "We must stop in Jerusalem and go to the temple. There we will give thanks for Jesus and dedicate Him to God."

So they did. And while they were there, an old man came in. His name was Simeon. He was a good man and very religious. He knew all about God's promise to send to the world a great King and Savior called the "Messiah." It had been revealed to him by the Holy Spirit that he would not die until he had seen this promised Savior. When Simeon saw Mary and Joseph and the baby Jesus, the Holy Spirit whispered to him again, "This is the child that will become God's Messiah."

He hurried over to Mary and Joseph. He asked if he might hold Jesus in his arms. Then he prayed: "Dear God, thank you for this moment. I am now ready to die because I have seen with my own eyes the Savior you have sent to bring light and peace to all the people."

Then he blessed Mary and Joseph. He told them that to be the Savior of the world, Jesus would later have to suffer many things. While many people would love Him, others would hate Him and seek to kill Him.

Simeon Thanks God for Jesus

Then, turning to Mary, he said, "You, too, later will be called upon to suffer as if a sword had pierced your own heart." Mary did not know what this meant at the time, but she did not forget it. She understood what it meant later when Jesus was crucified.

Just then a very religious woman, known as a prophetess, came over to where they were. Anna was her name, and she was eighty-four years old. When she saw Jesus, she, too, took Him into her arms and thanked God. Then she told the people close by that this child would be the Messiah of the nation and the Savior of the world.

Both Simeon and Anna returned to their homes with deep joy and gratitude in their hearts. Mary and Joseph were happy and grateful too, because their words had reminded them of what the shepherds and the Magi had said when Jesus was born.

As they left the temple, Joseph said to Mary: "God has truly blessed us with a very special little son! Let us continue to pray that He will grow up to be the kind of Savior the world needs."

"And when we get home," Mary added, "we must do our part to teach Him all the things He will need to know in order to be able to do all that God expects of Him."

With this purpose in their hearts, the next morning they started out again for their home in Nazareth. There Jesus continued to grow stronger and wiser day after day in a way that pleased God very much.

★ ★ ★ ★ ★ ★ ★ ★

Prayer

Dear God, thank You for everyone who loved me and said nice things about me when I was a little baby. Help me to be the kind of boy (or girl) that they will still love and say nice things about as I grow older. Help me to be what You want me to be. In Jesus' name, amen.

★ ★ ★ ★ ★ ★ ★ ★

QUESTIONS ON CHAPTER TWENTY-FIVE

1. In what way were you a "mixed blessing" to your parents when you were born?
2. Why did the "Wise-men" not return to their country by way of Jerusalem?
3. What did Herod do when he found out what they had done?
4. What did the angel tell Joseph to do?
5. On their way back from Egypt, what did Mary and Joseph do in Jerusalem?
6. What did Simeon do and say when he saw the baby Jesus?
7. What did Anna do and say?
8. How do you suppose Mary felt about Simeon's words about Jesus and about her? What do you think Joseph thought?
9. How do you suppose the other people in the temple felt about what Simeon and Anna said about Jesus?

Chapter Twenty-six

GROWING UP

Do you sometimes wish you could grow up faster than you do? A puppy becomes a dog in less than a year. In two years, a colt is as large as its father or mother and can outrace both of them!

Why does it take so much time for us human beings to become full grown? Could it be because we are so much more important to God than His other creatures?

An artist can draw a pen and pencil sketch of an object in a few minutes. But to produce a masterpiece in color requires many long hours of his time and skill!

So, maybe in the time it takes you to grow up, God wants to produce a masterpiece! Even Jesus had to grow from babyhood to manhood before He could be the Savior of the world.

Nazareth was a little town. It was the kind of town where everyone knew everyone else. It was so ordinary that some people said, "Can any good thing come out of Nazareth?"

But they were wrong! Many great and good

men have come out of very ordinary places. And Jesus came out of Nazareth!

He learned a great deal there in what might be called "the school of experience." He learned from what He did and what He saw. He learned by going places, too.

He learned the names of all living things that grew in the hills and valleys—the crops, the trees, the fruits, the mustard plants, the wheat, even the weeds. He knew the shepherds and often watched them caring for their sheep. He learned to share their concern for every lamb in their flock—particularly for one that might have gone astray. He knew the farmers in their fields. He watched them plowing, sowing, reaping, and storing their grain in the barns.

But experience was not the only school from which Jesus learned. At the age of six, He was enrolled in the village school. It was very different from the one you attend. It met in a Jewish church, called a synagogue, and the teacher was the minister of the synagogue, called a "rabbi."

There were no books, no desks, no chairs. The pupils sat in a circle on the floor as the rabbi taught them to repeat with him the ten commandments and other important passages from their sacred writings, known to us as the Old Testament. Jesus was a bright and attentive pupil and learned His lessons well; so He often quoted verses from the Old Testament and explained their meaning when He was a man.

Every Sabbath morning, He went with Mary and Joseph to the synagogue to worship God and to hear the rabbi speak.

From a child's viewpoint, the services were very dull, but Jesus did not use this as an excuse to stay away. He faithfully obeyed all the commandments, two of which are, "Remember the Sabbath day to keep it holy," and, "Honor thy father and thy mother."

When it was not the Sabbath and Jesus was not in school, He particularly enjoyed helping Joseph in his carpenter shop. One day, after a busy morning working together, Joseph took Jesus on a hike to the top of a mountain just outside Nazareth. There, under the shade of a tree, as they shared a picnic lunch Mary had prepared, they could see almost all of the province of Galilee. "Galilee" means "circle," and that is what it was—a round fertile valley surrounded by hills.

"That mountain over there, straight across the valley," said Joseph, pointing west, "is Mt. Carmel. That is where the prophet Elijah built an altar before the people of Israel, then called down lightning from Heaven that set fire to the sacrifice on the altar. Thus, he convinced the people of Israel that Jehovah was the true God whom they should worship and not Baal, the false god whom they had been worshiping."

159

Joseph Teaches Jesus

"And that mountain over there is Mt. Gilboa, where King Saul and his three sons died fighting bravely against the Philistines.

"After that, David became king," Joseph continued. "He was the most famous king our nation ever had."

Then, putting his arm around Jesus, Joseph said, "Jesus, your mother and I are both grateful and proud that David was one of Your ancestors. Our people are still hoping that God will send us a 'Messiah,' that is, a king who will be like David and also a descendant of David. And Your mother and I are praying that You will become that person when You are grown up."

No wonder Jesus loved Joseph as much as He loved His mother. And it's no wonder that what Joseph and Mary taught Jesus about God and the writings of the prophets in the Old Testament helped Him so much to understand the kind of Messiah God wanted Him to be when He was a full-grown man.

Yes, He had a bright mind, and His eyes and ears were open to all that happened around Him; so He learned much from the school of experience. And He was a diligent student in the synagogue school; so He learned much from His teachers, the rabbis. But His best teachers were His parents. They never forgot the visit of the shepherds and the Magi when He was born, nor the words of Simeon and Anna in the temple. They kept doing everything they could to prepare Him to become the person God sent Him into the world to be.

Of course Jesus did His part, too, by always being an attentive, obedient, and cooperative son. And both Mary and Joseph were proud of Him!

★ ★ ★ ★ ★ ★ ★ ★

Prayer

Dear God, I pray that, like Jesus, I may grow up to be the person you want me to be and do the things you want me to do.

Please help me to do my part every day to make this prayer come true. In Jesus' name, amen.

★ ★ ★ ★ ★ ★ ★ ★

QUESTIONS ON CHAPTER TWENTY-SIX

1. What was the school that Jesus attended like? Where did it meet? Who was the teacher?
2. Why do you think Jesus was a good student? What kind of student are you?
3. Where else did Jesus learn things?
4. Who were Jesus' best teachers?
5. How often did Jesus' family worship in the synagogue?
6. What do you want to do for God when you grow up? What are you doing for Him now?
7. How do you act when church services seem dull? How did Jesus act?

Chapter Twenty-seven

QUESTIONS AND ANSWERS

When you have questions that puzzle or trouble you—about God, about the Bible, about what is right and what is wrong, about what to do with your life—where do you go for an answer? To your father or mother? To one of your teachers? To the minister of your church?

When Jesus was a boy, where do you suppose He went for the answers to such questions?

★ ★ ★ ★ ★ ★ ★ ★

Jesus was almost too excited to sleep! All day long, He had helped His mother and Joseph get together the things they would need for their journey the next day. They were going to Jerusalem to celebrate the Passover.

The Passover was a religious festival observed by Jewish families once every year. It was an expression of their thanksgiving to God for delivering them from slavery in the land of Egypt many years before. Mary and

163

Joseph went to Jerusalem every year for this celebration. Jesus was now twelve years old; so for the first time, He was going too!

To Jerusalem! To worship God in His holy temple! The temple He had heard so much about in the synagogue school! The temple, where, as He had been told, His parents had taken Him when He was a baby and dedicated Him to God! The temple, where there were brilliant religious teachers who would be able to answer some of the questions that kept coming to His mind! No wonder Jesus was excited!

The next morning, with Mary and Joseph, He was up bright and early to start on the journey. There were many people going from Nazareth. They traveled together in what was called a caravan. They walked all day, sharing their food along the way, and they slept at night under the stars. Jerusalem was about sixty miles from Nazareth; so it took them three or four days to make the journey. When they stopped and made camp for the last night, they could see the walls of the city and the temple on the hills above them.

After supper, the people gathered for a vesper service. Facing toward the temple, they sang one of their familiar psalms (121).

"I to the hills will lift mine eyes,
Oh whence for me shall help arise?
From the Lord shall come my aid,
Who the heaven and earth hath made.

He will surely keep thy soul,
What would harm He will control,
He will keep thee day by day,
In the home and by the way."

The next morning, as the people entered the temple courtyard, Jesus was fascinated, but troubled, by what He saw. Money changers were everywhere, shouting to get attention and overcharging as they exchanged Roman coins for Jewish money. Merchants asked three times too much for the doves and lambs required for the sacrificial offerings!

All around were priests, hundreds of them, all living on the gifts the people brought to the temple. Why did the merchants charge so much for the animals? What did the priests do with the money? Why did they sacrifice animals on the altar? Was this all God expected and wanted of people? Were there not other things more important? What did God want most of all?

Jesus recalled some of the verses from the prophets He had heard and memorized in the synagogue school: " 'The multitude of your sacrifices—what are they to me?' says the Lord. 'I have more than enough of burnt offerings, of rams and the fat of fattened animals; I have no pleasure in the blood of bulls and lambs and goats' " (Isaiah 1:11, NIV).

"He has showed you, O man, what is good. And what does the Lord require of you? To act justly and to love mercy and to walk humbly with your God" (Micah 6:8, NIV).

Jesus wondered whether the prophets were right. If so, why all these offerings of animals on the altar? What was the heart of religion anyway?

These were some of the questions that kept going around in the mind of Jesus as He watched what was going on in the temple area. And He needed to know the answers if He was some day to be God's Messiah! This should be the place and the time to get the answers, for was not this His Father's house? And the questions were still there as He tried to sleep with the other people from Nazareth in the camp they had pitched on the outside of Jerusalem.

The next morning, it was decided that they would go back to the temple for one more worship service and then start for home. Later that morning, Jesus noticed a group of priests and religious teachers in a balcony of the temple. They had rolls of the Scriptures and were discussing and debating certain passages from the prophets. Perhaps here He could find the answers to some of His questions. Turning away from the crowd moving into the worship service, He joined the discussion group. He listened eagerly to everything that was being said. When He had a chance, He began asking questions himself.

Jesus and the Teachers Discuss Scripture

The learned doctors of religion were amazed that a boy so young could come up with such intelligent questions. Also, they were amazed by the answers He gave to some of their questions. On and on the discussion went, with both Jesus and the teachers so interested that they lost all sense of time.

It was very late when they stopped the discussion. Jesus slept alone in the temple so He could return early to the discussion the next day. He spent that whole day discussing the Scriptures with the priests and teachers. A second night He slept alone in the temple. On the third day, while Jesus was again involved in a discussion of the Scriptures with the temple scholars, Mary and Joseph rushed into the temple.

Throwing her arms around Jesus, Mary said with tears in her eyes: "Oh, my son, we thought You were lost! We have been looking everywhere for You! We supposed You were with some of our friends and relatives, but when we couldn't find You in the crowd returning to Nazareth, we came all the way back to look for You. Why did You treat us this way?"

Jesus was sorry about His mother's anxiety, but He was glad He had stayed to get the answers to some of His questions. So He said: "Why did you seek for Me somewhere else, Mother? Didn't you know I would be here in

My Father's house learning about My Father's business?''

Mary did not understand this strange answer at the time. But she kept thinking about it. The more she did, the more she realized that even at the age of twelve, Jesus was well on the way to becoming what God, His heavenly Father, had sent Him into the world to be—the promised Messiah and Savior of the world!

After that never-to-be-forgotten experience in the temple, Jesus went back to Nazareth with Mary and Joseph. There, through His teenage years, He continued to live as their dutiful son—growing, working, studying, listening, learning, and all the while thinking and praying more and more about His ''heavenly Father's business.''

He was loved and admired by all who knew Him. In due time, He was fully prepared to fulfill the purpose for which God had sent Him into the world.

Prayer

Dear God, like Jesus, I want to find and to fulfill the purpose You had in mind when You sent me into the world. I want to be the person You want me to be and to do the work You want me to do.

So help me to use my time, my opportunities, and my talents while I am growing up that I, too, may be fully prepared for what You want me to be and to do when I am fully grown. In Jesus' name, amen.

★ ★ ★ ★ ★ ★ ★ ★

QUESTIONS ON CHAPTER TWENTY-SEVEN

1. Why was the Passover celebration so important to Jewish families in the time of Jesus?

2. Why was Jesus eager to visit the temple in Jerusalem?

3. What did the people from Nazareth do on the last night before they arrived in Jerusalem?

4. What did Jesus see the people doing in the temple courtyard? Why was He troubled?

5. How would you have felt about the unfair things going on at the temple?

6. Why did the Jews offer sacrifices? What do you think the words of the prophets meant?

7. What did Jesus do about the questions in His mind? What did the religious teachers think about Him?

8. How do you feel about asking questions? Whom do you ask when you want to know something about the Bible?

9. What did Mary say when she and Joseph found Jesus in the temple?

10. What do you think Jesus meant when He answered Mary? What is God's business?

Chapter Twenty-eight

DOING GOD'S THING

Some young people, we are told, leave home because they get "fed up" and decide they want to "do their own thing." In the Bible, there is a story about a young man who left home because He "looked up" and decided He wanted to "do God's thing."

★ ★ ★ ★ ★ ★ ★ ★

As you may recall, when Jesus was twelve years old, He went with Mary and Joseph to Jerusalem for the Passover celebration. After His unforgettable experience in the temple there, He spent the next eighteen years of His life in Nazareth. There, day after day, He worked with Joseph in the carpenter shop and thus helped to support the family. There were several younger children in the family besides himself.

When Jesus was thirty years old, He realized the time had come for Him to move out into the world and to tend to His "heavenly Father's business."

Then He thought of His cousin, John, known as "John the Baptizer." He knew God had sent John to prepare the people for

His own coming. So He decided to go to John to be baptized.

In some ways, John was a strange man. He lived in a cave in the desert. His hair and beard were long. His food was locusts and wild honey. The clothing he wore was a rough cloak made from the hide of a camel, with a leather cord around his waist.

But he was really a powerful preacher! His eyes flashed like flames of fire, and his voice was deep like the roll of thunder as he shouted, "Repent, turn away from your sins! For the kingdom of Heaven is near, and God's Messiah is coming soon."

Up and down near the River Jordan he went, preaching to the throngs who came. And they did come, from miles around, to see him and to hear what he had to say.

People listened spellbound to his words, and hundreds confessed their sins and were baptized by him in the River Jordan. So impressed were they by his eloquence and by the multitudes that followed him that they said to one another: "Perhaps this man is the Messiah."

But John said, "No! After me is coming one much greater than I. I am only a voice crying in the wilderness. I am the one Isaiah the prophet was speaking about when he wrote: 'Prepare the way for the Lord. Make a straight path for His coming.' The one God is sending is so much greater than I that I am not even worthy to stoop down and untie His sandals. I can only baptize with water, but He will baptize with the Holy Spirit."

But while John was sure the Messiah was about to come and that He would be a very great man, he did not know who He was to be. So he prayed for God to give him a sign. God's answer was, "When you see the Holy Spirit coming down from Heaven in the form of a dove and resting upon a man, that is the Messiah."

Not long after that, Jesus came to the River Jordan and asked John to baptize Him. When John saw Him coming, he recognized Him immediately—that is he recognized Him as his cousin, Jesus. Though they had grown up in homes some sixty miles apart, once in a while they had met at Passover time in Jerusalem or at a family reunion; so they knew one another. And now, as Jesus came nearer, the Holy Spirit whispered to John: "This is the Lamb of God. He will take away the sins of the world."

In a flash, John realized that God had sent Jesus to be the Savior and the Messiah. So he said to Jesus: "I am not worthy to baptize You; it should be the other way around. You should baptize me."

But Jesus replied: "No, John, this is the way it should be. I want to show that I approve of the message you are preaching and that people are doing the right thing when

John Prepares to Baptize Jesus

they confess their sins, turn away from them, and are baptized."

Then they went down to the river together, and John did baptize Jesus. After they came up out of the water, and as Jesus was kneeling on the bank praying, sure enough, as God had promised, the Holy Spirit came down from Heaven in the form of a dove and rested on Jesus' shoulder. John saw it clearly; then he knew for certain that Jesus was the Messiah God had promised. The sign he had prayed for had been given!

But that was not all that happened while Jesus was praying. A voice was heard from Heaven saying: "You are my own dear Son, and I am greatly pleased with You."

Those words were spoken to encourage Jesus and to make Him strong in the face of the trials and temptations that lay ahead. In effect, God was saying: "So far, so good, my dear Son. You have made a good beginning and have made me very happy. Carry on! Carry on!"

★ ★ ★ ★ ★ ★ ★ ★

Prayer

Dear God, like Jesus, I don't want to do "*my* thing," but "*Your* thing." So this is my prayer and promise:

I'll go where you want me to go,
O'er mountain, or plain, or sea;
I'll do what you want me to do,
I'll be what you want me to be.

Just as I am, young, strong and free;
To be the best that I can be
For truth and righteousness and Thee,
Lord of my life, I come.

In Jesus' name, amen.

★ ★ ★ ★ ★ ★ ★ ★

QUESTIONS ON CHAPTER TWENTY-EIGHT

1. Why did Jesus decide to leave His home in Nazareth? How old was He?
2. What was the first thing He did after leaving home?
3. Describe John the Baptizer.
4. When he preached, what did he call upon the people to do?
5. What did he say to people who thought he might be the Messiah?
6. What sign did God promise to give him?
7. What did John say when Jesus asked to be baptized?
8. What was Jesus' reply?
9. Describe what happened after Jesus was baptized.
10. What did the voice from Heaven say?
11. If God spoke to you as He did to Jesus, would He say He was pleased or unhappy? What can you do to please God?

Chapter Twenty-nine

THE LITTLE LUNCH THAT WENT A LONG WAY

Perhaps you have heard the fable about the lion caught in a trap. The hunters planned to carry him to the king; so they bound him tightly with a rope, tied him to a tree, and went to get a wagon.

While they were gone, along came the mouse who was a friend of the lion. With his sharp teeth, he gnawed and gnawed on the rope until it broke in two, and the lion was set free!

That fable reminds us that one does not have to be big to do something important. There is a story in the Bible that tells us that, too.

★ ★ ★ ★ ★ ★ ★ ★

The dust and sand went sailing through the door as Rachel vigorously pushed her reed broom over the floor of her modest home on the side of the hill close to the Sea of Galilee. Already she had pulled aside the curtain hanging over the window to let in the light of the sun.

Her husband, Daniel, was a carpenter and had left for work an hour earlier. But first he had helped their six-year-old Joel put together his simple fishing equipment. Joel and two of his little friends had often "tried their luck" from the dock at the foot of the hill, and today they were going again. Rachel had packed him a little lunch and sent him on his joyful way an hour after Daniel had left. Her face was bright with a smile as she watched him going down the path, clutching his fishing rod in one hand and his lunch bag in the other.

"Be careful," she called. "Remember to stay on the dock, and don't forget we want some nice fresh fish for supper." She and Daniel knew the lake well. Often they had played on the sandy shore and waded in its cool shallow water when they were little. In Joel's happy care-free spirit, they were reliving their own childhood.

Both of them were proud of their son—his healthy body, his bright mind, his dancing brown eyes, his mop of curly brown hair. Their one concern was that now and then as he played with his friends, he seemed selfish and inconsiderate, unwilling to share, greedy. "But he will outgrow it," they said to one another, and they hoped and prayed that it would be so.

Soon after she had finished putting her house in order, Rachel picked up her water jar and headed for the village well. There she met two of her friends, Deborah and Miriam, who had also come to draw water. As they filled their jars, they shared with one another items of news about their village and the world outside. On this particular morning, Deborah could hardly wait to share with them her big item of news.

"Last night, my husband heard through a fisherman friend whose name is Zebedee that the famous rabbi, Jesus from Nazareth, is on the other side of the lake with a great crowd following Him. Two of His twelve disciples are sons of Zebedee, and they think He may come over to our side of the lake some time today."

"But why would He come over to our little village?" asked Miriam. "There are so many more people on the other side of the lake."

"That is just the reason," answered Deborah. "According to Zebedee, over there the crowds are so large that He needs to rest."

"It sounds too good to be true," said Rachel, her eyes bright with expectation. Then she thought of Daniel. The house he was helping to build was close to theirs, but higher on the hill. From that point, he would be able to see far out into the lake and watch for any boat that might be approaching. She told her friends she would go and tell him. So the three of them picked up their water jars and hurried home.

Daniel, too, was excited by the news Rachel reported and promised to keep watching the lake. But he said he didn't think any rabbi as famous as Jesus of Nazareth would ever visit their little village.

Before long, Deborah's report was the one topic of conversation all over the town. Excitement and hope were spreading like wildfire!

Just before noon, Daniel came down from the hill and reported, first to Rachel and then to the townspeople, that he had indeed seen a boat coming across the lake. "Also," he said, "from the top of the hill, I saw a big crowd walking around the lake, coming this way. Lots of the people with Jesus on the other side of the lake seem to be following Him over here."

Soon the whole village was on the move as men, women, and children hurried down to the dock where the boat was pulling in. Shouts of welcome were heard as Jesus, followed by His twelve disciples, stepped ashore. Two of the recognized leaders of the community greeted them warmly and asked Jesus to stay and teach them as He had done for the people on the other side of the lake. So Jesus, although He was quite weary, invited the people to follow Him up the hill. There He would teach them.

As Rachel and Daniel walked up the hill together, she suddenly thought of Joel.

"Where do you suppose he is?" she said to Daniel. "The boat came into the very dock where he was supposed to be fishing, but I did not see him anywhere."

"Don't worry," Daniel replied. "He's good at taking care of himself. Besides, everybody in the village knows him. He'll be all right."

By the time Jesus began to teach, the crowd had grown to several thousand because of the hundreds who had walked around the lake from the other side. And how intently they all listened! Never had they heard such words before!

Words about God's loving care: "Look at the birds flying and singing under the blue sky. God takes care of them, and you mean more to Him than they do. So do not worry about anything. Trust your heavenly Father, and He will supply all your needs."

Words about faith and prayer: "Ask and you will receive; seek and you will find; knock and the door will open. If you parents find joy in giving good gifts to your children, surely your Father in Heaven will not fail to give good gifts to you, His children, if you ask Him."

Words about unselfishness and love: "Treat others as you want them to treat you. Remember there is more joy in giving than in getting."

He had spoken for nearly an hour, when

suddenly Daniel and Rachel spied Joel. He was standing not far from Jesus. In fact, he was right beside one of Jesus' disciples. His fishing rod was on the ground beside him, and at his feet was his lunch bag. Apparently, he had become so excited that he had forgotten about the lunch.

His eyes were fixed on Jesus. Joel was drinking in every word as Jesus said: "Come to me, all of you who are tired and who have heavy burdens to carry, and I will give you rest. Bring to me your little children, too, that I may bless them. For to them belongs the kingdom of God. I say to you, anyone who does not come to God with the loving trust of a little child will not enter His kingdom."

By now, it was getting late, and Jesus came to the close of His message. As He finished, He blessed the people in God's name. As the people lingered, they could see He was talking quietly with His disciples.

Then one of them, the one who had been beside Joel—his name was Andrew—stepped forward and announced: "Our Master knows you are hungry and He wants you to have something to eat before you go home. Do you have any food you would be willing to share with one another?"

The people looked at each other in amazement! What a strange request! Away out here on the hillside in late afternoon—who could possibly have any food?

But, unnoticed by anyone except his father and mother and a few people close to Andrew, Joel was stepping forward. Holding out his bag to Andrew, he said: "Here is my lunch. I will share it with someone."

"Well, well, my little man," said Andrew, "how generous of you! Let's see what's inside." Then, looking into the bag, he said, "Not a very big lunch, is it? But let's take it to Jesus."

So they walked over to where Jesus was. "Master," said Andrew, "this little boy has brought his lunch—five barley rolls and two little fish. He wants to share it, but, of course, this couldn't begin to feed this crowd."

"Andrew," said Jesus, "you must not forget, with God all things are possible. Have the people sit down."

As Andrew and the other disciples did as Jesus said, Jesus took the lunch from Joel's hand. He thanked Joel for giving it, and He asked God to bless it and to make it more and more so all the people could eat. After His prayer, He began to break the rolls and fish into small pieces and to pass them to His disciples. They, in turn, shared with the people and the people with one another. The more they shared, the more there was to share—until all had eaten as much as they wanted. Not one went away hungry!

Not even Joel, because he too had eaten as

Joel Shares His Lunch

much as he wanted. Also, he was happier than he had ever been before! Why? Because he had learned in his own experience how true it is: "There is more joy in giving than in getting."

★ ★ ★ ★ ★ ★ ★ ★

Prayer

Dear God, I am never happy when I am selfish. So whether I have much or little, teach me the joy of sharing. In Jesus' name, amen.

★ ★ ★ ★ ★ ★ ★ ★

QUESTIONS ON CHAPTER TWENTY-NINE

1. What was Daniel and Rachel's one concern about Joel?

2. Why did Jesus go from one side of the lake to the other?

3. What are some of the things Joel heard Jesus say?

4. What did Joel do when Andrew asked whether anyone had some food to share?

5. Have you ever felt you were not important because you were small? What have you learned from this story about that?

6. What do you suppose Joel thought when he offered his lunch to Andrew?

7. What do you think he thought after Jesus fed all those people with his lunch?

8. What do you think he learned about selfishness? What have *you* learned about selfishness?

Chapter Thirty

THE MEASURE OF A MAN

Mr. Edgar A. Guest once wrote a poem in answer to his little boy's question, "Daddy, when will I be a man?" Here is his answer.

"When shall I be a man?" he said
As I was putting him to bed.
"How many years will have to be
Before time makes a man of me?"
. . . I heaved a sigh,
Because it called for careful thought
To give the answer that he sought.

And so I sat him on my knee,
And said to him: "A man you'll be
When you have learned that honor brings
More joy than all the crowns of kings;
That it is better to be true
To all who know and trust in you
Than all the gold of earth to gain,
If winning it shall leave a stain . . .

When you are kind and brave and clean,
And fair to all and never mean;
When there's good in all you plan.
That day, my boy, you'll be a man."

The Bible tells us a story about a man who was rich and successful, but who was not a real man until one never-to-be-forgotten day.

★ ★ ★ ★ ★ ★ ★ ★

"How could any man have so much and yet be so unhappy?" Zaccheus kept asking himself as he rested on his couch in his elegant home in Jericho. He was one of the richest Jews in the city. But he had hardly any friends and was very lonely.

As he thought back to the time he was a child, he realized that even then he was seldom happy. He had been small for his age—undersized! So he was left out of games and not invited to parties. How often he had heard, "He's too little!"

"Shorty" had been his nickname. His real name, *Zaccheus,* meant "righteous" or "just." That was a nice name. But "Shorty" was just awful!

So he had given up trying to make friends and had become more and more a loner, jealous of others and resentful, holding in his anger and wishing for some way to get even with those who made fun of him!

Now, as a man, he had found a way. He was still a "Shorty," less than five feet tall. But he was a tax collector. In that position, he found a devilish delight in collecting taxes from his former schoolmates who had left him out of their games and called him "Shorty." Many times he had charged more than was due, and, thus, had become richer and richer.

But from another point of view, he had become poorer and poorer. The few friends he had cared for him less and less, while his enemies hated him more and more. Behind his back, and sometimes to his face, they called him "Swindler." He hated that nickname even more than "Shorty," but he really deserved it because of the way he cheated people on their taxes. They also called him "Traitor" because he collected taxes for the Romans. No wonder he felt so lonely and unhappy as he rested on his soft couch.

His troubled thoughts were suddenly interrupted by loud shouting not far away. He sent a servant to find out what was the cause. A few minutes later, the servant came back and reported that a famous rabbi by the name of Jesus, with a band of twelve disciples, was approaching.

"He is on His way to Jerusalem to celebrate the Passover feast," said the servant. "A large crowd is gathered on both sides of the street to see Him pass by."

"I have heard of Him," said Zaccheus. "I must see Him, too." So he arose from his couch and hurried out. But when he reached the main street, he could not see over the heads of the crowd. No one made way for him or even spoke to him.

So he ran on ahead to a sycamore tree beside the street. Reaching one of the limbs, he climbed to a point several feet above the crowd. Now he had what might be called a "ringside" seat, where he could see everything and would be noticed by no one.

As Jesus came near, Zaccheus noticed the strength of His stride, His noble face, and the warmth of His smile. No wonder the people were so enthusiastic! How fortunate were those twelve strong men walking close to Him to be His disciples! He almost wished he were one of them.

And then Jesus was passing right under the tree! But no! Not passing! He was stopping! Looking up into the tree, Jesus called him by name! "Zaccheus!" He said. "Come down! Hurry! I am going home with you!"

Zaccheus could not believe his ears! Never before had anyone spoken to him like that. None of his neighbors or business acquaintances had ever expressed a wish to visit him in his home. For years, he had been ignored, laughed at, rejected, and despised by the Jews for being a tax collector for the Romans.

And now, all of a sudden, here was this famous, popular rabbi saying in effect, "Of all the people in Jericho, you are the one I would like to know."

Of course, Zaccheus hurried down from the tree! Of course, he welcomed Jesus warmly! He did it "with great joy," the Bible

Zaccheus Sees Jesus

says. He was happier than he had ever been as they walked together toward his home! He heard some of the people murmuring about Jesus' going home with the big swindler, but he was too happy to care!

The Bible does not tell us what they talked about that night. Possibly Zaccheus found the courage to tell Jesus how unhappy he had been all his life because he was undersized. Perhaps he told Jesus how unhappy he still was in spite of his wealth.

And perhaps Jesus quietly told him how much good he could do for poor people with his wealth, and that his real problem was not his size, but his attitude—that he had allowed himself to become resentful and unforgiving, selfish and greedy—that it was what was inside that was making him miserable, not what was outside.

While we do not know what Jesus said to him as they talked together, we do know that as a result, Zaccheus became a different man! Before they retired for the night, he said to Jesus, "Right away, I am going to give half of my wealth to the poor, and if I have over-charged anyone on his taxes, I will give him back four times as much."

Then and there, Zaccheus turned his life around and became a new and noble person. Jesus said "salvation" had come to Zaccheus and added that He, Jesus, had come into the world "to seek and to save the lost." That means that Zaccheus, once lost and unhappy because of his anger, selfishness, and greed, had now put all of these feelings out of his heart and allowed Jesus to come in instead.

★ ★ ★ ★ ★ ★ ★ ★

Prayer
Dear God, keep me from being hurt or angry toward anyone who may mistreat me or make fun of me. And help me always to treat others, especially those who may be mistreated or neglected, as I, myself, like to be treated. Make me thoughtful and kind as Jesus was. In Jesus' name, amen.

★ ★ ★ ★ ★ ★ ★ ★

QUESTIONS ON CHAPTER THIRTY

1. Why was Zaccheus so unhappy?
2. What does the name *Zaccheus* mean?
3. How did Zaccheus "get even" with those who had been mean to him when he was a boy?
4. Why couldn't Zaccheus see Jesus as He passed through Jericho? What did he do about it?
5. Why do you think Jesus wanted to go home with Zaccheus?
6. What do you suppose they talked about that night?
7. How do you know Zaccheus became a changed man?
8. In what ways do you need to be changed?
9. How can Jesus do for you what He did for Zaccheus?

192